It's all Geek to Me

Effective communication for the technically minded

By Paul LaPointe

Edited by John Dias

Version 2.00

Copyright 2014 Paul LaPointe
All rights reserved
Printed in the United States of America
Second Edition
ISBN 978-0-9937891-0-6

No part of this publication may be reproduced, distributed, or transmitted in any form or by any means, or stored in a database or retrieval system, without the prior written permission of the publisher.

Contents

Forward	iv
Release Notes	vi
Chapter 1: Chinese Graffiti	1
Chapter 2: Roads less travelled	23
Chapter 3: Why should communication matter to Geeks?	33
Chapter 4: How rational is your thinking?	49
Chapter 5: Consistency and Bias	61
Chapter 6: The Audience	75
Chapter 7: Channel Capacity	87
Chapter 8: Effective Listening	99
Chapter 9: Plan to fail to avoid failing	109
Chapter 10: What's the point?	115
Chapter 11: Noise	125
Chapter 12: Choosing the *right* medium for the message	141
Chapter 13: The Six Sins of Communication	149
Chapter 14: Perspectives on truth	165
Chapter 15: Telling the Truth	175
Chapter 16: Influencing people	187
Chapter 17: Confidence	199
Chapter 18: Conclusion	203
Bibliography	207
Acknowledgements	209
About the Author	211

Foreword

I had the pleasure of working with Paul at xkoto, our fledgling software start-up from its founding in 2005 to acquisition in 2010. As you will read in these pages, Paul has the "cred" to speak authoritatively on the challenges and opportunities for geeks to communicate more effectively. Paul was part of our development team when he was tapped to take a customer-facing role as a pre-sales engineer. Together, we learned a lot about how to express complex concepts to wide-ranging audiences.

This book captures practical lessons learned in the trenches, presented with a dry wit and insight earned the hard way. If you are a geek you may resist the suggestions that follow as "exercises for the reader", but I suggest you give the content a chance – it may change the quality of your relationships with colleagues and significant others. If you are not a geek, you will find that this book serves well as a primer on understanding how geeks communicate (or don't) so that you too can gain more in your dealings with "the dark side". Either way, as Paul points out, communication is a two way street – with the help of this book, maybe we can all walk on the same side for a change.

Albert Lee

Author of *How to Meet the Queen – Ask Good Questions, Get Good Answers*

Release Notes

Version 1.00 – June 2014
- Initial version.

Version 1.02 – Aug 2014
- Various spelling, grammar and reference corrections throughout the book.

Version 2.0 – Feb 2016
- Various grammar corrections throughout the book.
- Reformatted paragraphs to not break pages.
- Expanded content in Chapter 8: Effective Listening. Previously, this chapter was titled 'Active Listening'
- Expanded content in Chapter 12: Choosing the right medium for the message.
- Expanded content in Chapter 16: Influencing people

Chinese graffiti, all over town,
Chinese graffiti don't make a sound
- *"Chinese graffiti"* by Blue Peter, "Up to You", Ready Records, 1982

Chapter 1: Chinese Graffiti

"It's all Greek to me" is a phrase my father-in-law is fond of muttering whenever he can't follow what someone is saying. It might be used occasionally when the topic is too hard to follow, but more often than not it's said when the person speaking is too hard to follow. It's a nice, self-deprecating way of saying, "I have no clue what you are saying."

It's interesting that "It's all Greek to me" is an English idiom taken from Shakespeare. Different parts of the world have very similar phrases, but with their own local pick of which foreign language they believe to be the least comprehensible. In Italy, they might say that someone who is confusing is "speaking Arabic". If you happen to be in the Indian state of Maharashtra, and you don't make sense, people might say you are "speaking Kannad" (referring to the Indian state of Karnataka). And in Africa, Europe, and most of the rest of the world, Chinese becomes the incomprehensible tongue. You might also ask, what do people in China say when they can't understand someone's writing? Well, they might say that it's *chicken intestines*.

If someone claims you are speaking Greek (unless you are genuinely speaking Greek), what they are really saying is that you are not effectively communicating and you might as well be saying nothing. The use of the idiom, "It's all Greek to me" and all its variations might not last into the next few decades. The languages and tongues that were strange and incomprehensible to our parents are no match for our handy gadgets like smart phones that can offer instant translations of Cantonese into English. Web pages written in Arabic can also be transformed into Spanish with the click of a button. The world of human communication is poised for a revolution in understanding; but there's one very ironic catch to all this.

Although these amazing technologies and gadgets make it easier to communicate in the world, many of the people that create and contribute to these advances, the Geeks of the world, remain inscrutable and hard to understand. This doesn't need to be the case however. I believe with the right communication skills, Geeks can effectively communicate to make themselves and any idea they want to convey understandable.

This is a book on effective communication, written specifically for Geeks, by a self-professed Geek. If you're reading this, you probably know if you are a geek or not. For the rest of you that are not geeks, Wikipedia can supply a nice definition:

"The word 'geek' is a slang term originally used to describe eccentric or non-mainstream people, with different connotations ranging from "an expert or enthusiast" to "a person heavily interested in a hobby", with a general pejorative meaning of "a peculiar or otherwise dislikable person, especially one who is perceived to be overly intellectual".[1]

This is a relatively modern definition for the term Geek. It's a term that has enjoyed a significant evolution in the past two decades, as has the social perception of the people the term is generally applied to. Not so long ago, "Geek" was purely a derogatory term, referring to a performer in a circus show. Today, as Wikipedia's definition tells us, the "Geek" label is typically stuck to, or chosen by, people that have a keen interest in things that popular culture does not necessarily understand or accept.

It's not hard to see why the social perception of Geeks is slowly changing. Science and technology, while not quite cool, clearly have become fairly important in today's world. Geeks might not have attained coolness in the eyes of popular culture, but smart phones, social media sites, and other electronic gadgets, largely created by Geeks, have without question. Geeks have been brought into the focus of pop culture, as their inventions have become ubiquitous. Now pop culture is trying to make sense of geeks.

"Effective communication" is a pretty sterile term. It simply means saying or writing something so it can be understood by others. Many people tend to think communication skills are only relevant to public speaking, or perhaps writing a book. Some would (incorrectly) assume that this is the sort of skill naturally sought by those extroverted personalities who want to make a good first impression, or have ambitions to climb a corporate ladder. I hope you'll feel by the end of this book that this is not the case. Learning to communicate effectively is something that everyone needs and benefits from. It is critical for those in positions what we don't immediately think of as "social", like a computer programmer, scientist or engineer. In fact it is as important for them as it is for people with clearly social positions like a salesperson, manager or teacher. People who sit by themselves and never leave their desk need to learn how to express themselves as much as those who spend all day addressing large crowds of people.

Communicating well is not always an easy task. It's easy to find examples when it's *not* being done well. Earlier in my career, I worked in the Canadian nuclear industry, as part of a group that did computer modeling of nuclear reactors for training. The group, naturally, was made up of geeks. Many were physicists and engineers with PhDs. Some had multiple PhDs. It was a very brainy collection of geeks. As in most IT related workplaces, the people in the room were a pretty ethnically and culturally diverse group. Some had immigrated to Canada from China, India, the Middle East and Africa.

One day, the company brought in a new vice-president to head our department — an American, originally from Georgia who had been working in the nuclear industry in the U.S. and was new to Canada. He had the challenging task of addressing the department to explain a new series of organizational changes meant to improve the effectiveness of our department. He began by drawing a comparison between the business, and a recent NFL game featuring his favorite team, the Tampa Bay Buccaneers. Eyes in the room immediately glassed over. American football was not popular with this crowd, and we were a long way from Tampa Bay. I'm sure no one in the room had seen the game in question. At some point, he moved on to baseball. This might have worked a little better, but was certainly not winning the crowd over.

As TV shows like 'The Big Bang Theory' suggest, physicists and engineers tend not to have as much interest in sports as the general public. The new vice-president concluded with a few comparisons of our business to the war in Iraq. Had I been watching the meeting on television, I would have smacked myself in the head at this point. In a group with many cultural backgrounds, this was not a smart move. Some of the older members of the audience had been part of the peace movement in the 60s, and had strong views on the war. Some had emigrated from the Middle East, and had a strong emotional reaction to the subject. Finally, the vice-president wished us all a happy thanksgiving (which of course, had already passed, since it is celebrated a month earlier in Canada than in the U.S.).

The man's speech stuck with me because it was one of the worst public speaking disasters I had ever witnessed. In his efforts to build a relationship with his audience, he in fact isolated them. Some left the room openly hostile and annoyed. I heard one older colleague muttering under his breath in Mandarin. I'm fairly certain he was not saying something polite. The speaker had, in essence, been speaking the wrong language for his audience. This was a shame. I'm sure he did not intend to alienate himself from the group, but he didn't take the time to develop a sense of who he was speaking to.

Communication problems are not unique to Geeks, but Geeks usually share some common traits that pose challenges to effective communication. We'll examine how the interests of geeks can present some challenges for them. We'll see that geeks often have a tougher time communicating because they are usually inclined towards complex or technical subjects that other people find hard to understand.

Why Geeks need to communicate successfully is one of the first topics we'll discuss. Then in chapter two, we'll see what's in it for Geeks. But first, let's consider why the world needs Geeks who can communicate well.

This book's purpose

The world needs geeks who are articulate communicators. We

live in a world where technology, the bailiwick of geeks everywhere, touches almost every part of our lives. People share their entire lives, sometimes with complete strangers, on Facebook, LinkedIn, and Google+. Families and friends communicate without a second thought over email, using networking technology that two decades ago would only have been available in universities, large defense contractors, and large financial institutions. At some point, we started living in the future we dreamed of as children, and our parents likely never imagined.

Physical money, a part of human culture for thousands of years, is steadily being antiquated by electronic transactions. This can be a little unsettling to our primitive brain when you think about it. Our ancestors traded labor and physical goods for other labor and physical goods. Now, instead of a loaf of bread, or an acre of land, our "wealth" is determined by a set of electronic records, a particular arrangement of electrical fields sitting on disks inside large databases of our banks.

It's not just our financial system or our ways of doing commerce that have radically changed. It's our social nature. In all honesty, I had trouble making friends as a child. There were not enough kids around during my childhood with similar interests. Today, on the other hand, my young nephews make friends easily with other young teens in Italy, the UK, Germany, and other places (physically) far across the ever-shrinking planet.

I live next to a very nice elderly couple that I frequently enjoy speaking to. We often discuss how hard it is for me to be away from my wife and young baby since I travel a lot for my job. I've also heard about the couple's past. During World War II, the husband was stationed at an army base on the west coast. His young wife was at home in Toronto, and pregnant with their son. They kept in touch, over telegraph messages and letters (censored by the army of course) every few weeks. On the surface, both the couple and my family have experienced separation.

But truthfully, I can't comprehend what their experience was like. When I'm on the road, I Skype with my wife and daughter every night, and we often text each other throughout the day. It's impossible to understate the fact that this is not the same world that our parents grew up in, and it is utterly unrecognizable from the world my elderly neighbors grew up in. All of this change is due to technology.

It's not all sunshine and roses, of course. This technological world presents new problems and dangers that previous generations never imagined, let alone encountered. How could we have predicted 40 years ago that cyber bullying would be a leading cause of teen suicide? Or that, thieves on one side of the world would be breaking in to personal computers to obtain bank account and credit card information from unsuspecting victims on the other side? Updating one's relationship status to 'Single' on social networking sites can be a sure way to trigger the end of a marriage. In fact, "cyber-cheating"– or online flirting, is now a leading factor cited in divorce courts.

In the legal world, there are powerful corporate groups, like the MPAA and the RIAA, that are working to fundamentally redefine property laws that have essentially been part of human culture for literally thousands of years. Do you know that CD you own? Guess what ...maybe you don't actually own it. Maybe when you paid for it, you just paid for a license to *use* it (at least for a specified period of a time, decided by the record companies, and under very specific conditions, and only in sanctioned playback devices provided by specific companies). That shiny new tablet computer on your desk? Ditto...maybe instead of owning it, you only own a *license* to use it (but only as long as you don't open it, or try to figure out how it works, or use it in a way that certain groups don't approve of). Perhaps the real ownership of the computer is withheld to the corporation that build the hardware, or maybe the one that put the software on it. Technology has blurred even the simplest concepts of commerce.

The oldest and most constant human institution, war, has likewise been transformed by technology. Human soldiers are no longer even necessary. Why send a pilot to bomb an enemy when you can send a robot for a tenth of the price? Or ten robots for the same price? What happens when you can conduct war without the danger of losing any lives on your side? What happens when both sides start using robot drones and all the deaths are civilian deaths? Technology is posing some scary questions these days. Cory Doctorow, influential geek activist and science fiction author, put it this way: "We are living in a world where we no longer make airplanes, or cars. We are living in a world where we make computers with wings, and computers with wheels"[1]. Sophisticated technology now touches every part of our lives, from the moment we wake up, through the hours of the night while we sleep.

We could spend an entire book, or even several possible books, just discussing how technology impacts our lives. I don't think that would be of much interest to anyone; unless you are living in a cave, it's something you likely already know. We take for granted that technology has an impact on our world on a global level, and in our daily lives. It's clear the impact of technology is ubiquitous. But, how comprehensible is the technological world to normal people? I think the answer is unfortunately, not so much.

On the surface, the situation is not so bad. There are many social impacts of technology that have been obvious. Many of these are still unfolding. A few years prior to the writing of this book, the new force of social media helped trigger a turbulent era change. In the Middle East, regimes in Egypt, Libya, and Syria that had been stable for decades were over thrown into chaos as common people used the power of social media to organize and overthrow governments. In the USA, activists launched the 'Occupy movement'. Where I live in Canada, aboriginal groups launched an "Idle no more" movement modeled on the Occupy movement. You might consider these social upheavals positive or negative. There are some things this new era of high tech has brought us that are genuinely positive. For example, most of the world now has free access to the online encyclopedia Wikipedia. Similarly, the online Kahn academy provides free education classes on almost every topic imaginable.

I believe the average person is likely to recognize and understand how these things will change their lives. These effects of technology are all relatively immediate and obvious consequences of

---

[1] Cory Doctor, Dec 2011 lecture on "The coming war on general computation".

advances in communication and computer technology. In many ways, they can be described in a positive light, because they've made it easier for people to organize and take action. However, there is now a second wave emerging. These changes will be harder to recognize, and many of them will not be positive.

At the time I'm writing this book, the world's public is suddenly coming to the realization that every developed government in the world is actively spying on all the citizens and leaders of every other country in the world. Governments have justified this to their citizens under the guise of stopping terrorists, and dismissed concerns by downplaying the significance of the data actually collected. Strolling through a park recently, I heard two old ladies arguing on a bench about what *Metadata* was.

Young adults are slowly coming to realize that teenage indiscretions and inappropriate comments posted on the internet may never disappear, and may come back to haunt them years later when they apply for a job. Cheating spouses are slowly coming to realize that their smart phones can be turned against them by jealous spouses. Women and men are suddenly realizing that racy photos they have on their home computers might not be safe from outside eyes. This list could go on for a long time.

It's not just limited to technology involving electronics. Here's another example. I'm a recent father, so issues involving babies are fresh on my mind. If you buy baby bottles and toys today, you'll see the label BPA FREE displayed proudly on anything made with plastic. BisPhenol A is a compound used to make plastics clear and tough. It used to be a common ingredient in children's products. In the body, it's been found BisPhenol A mimics a hormone, and has been linked to a variety of human illnesses, including obesity, so many companies have voluntarily removed it. While doing so, they've also taken the opportunity to turn a bad thing into a positive marketing item by advertising their products as BPA FREE. Unfortunately, many of the compounds they have substituted for BisPhenol A also imitate hormones in the body, and may in fact be much worse for human health. The moral of this story is that what people do not understand about technology in the world today can hurt them.

On a global scale, scientists have warned the world that our emissions of greenhouse gases are changing our climate. Rather than acting in response to these warnings, Politicians, media pundits, and the general public have spent a decade debating exactly what scientists are really saying. This leads to the question of how can scientists efficiently share their messages without others manipulating and distorting it. Science and technology are definitely fields geeks are involved in. So where are the geeks in the discussions of how science and technology are changing our world? Are they spear-heading social understanding and change? Leading major companies? Holding elected office to help shape public policy? If the things geeks make and work with are so important, can we say that geeks have a substantial influence on the world? Sadly, I think the answer is probably "no".

Ask the average person, and you'll find they can name far more professional athletes, movie stars and musicians, let alone politicians, than scientists, programmers or engineers. Charities do not seek famous engineers to be their spokespersons. You don't seek any Nobel Prize winning chemists coming out with their own brand of perfume (although, that might make perfect sense - L'eau de Buckminster). But more seriously, if you look at the background of most of the men and women in US congress, or in parliament in the UK, you will find almost none with a technical background. Mark Henderson explores this problem in his book, *The Geek Manifesto*, and explains some of its unfortunate consequences. The boardrooms of most corporations are also lacking technical people. Geeks typically don't do much better in business than they do in politics, even though most business activity today is highly involved with technology.

The most common characteristic of CEOs in America is not technical literacy. It's *height*. Studies have consistently shown the average CEO is significantly taller than the average person. This offers an insight into how well our primitive brains are adapted to the modern world. Height should not be an evolutionary advantage today (we don't need to be very tall to reach things, we have ladders now.) But in some deep wired part of the brain, we equate someone being tall with being a good leader. Tall people therefore tend to end up as leaders.

The definition of a geek from Wikipedia does not mention anything about geeks being leaders, because they generally aren't in leadership positions. People don't see them as potential leaders, and worse, geeks don't see themselves as leaders. I think this is deeply unfortunate, because most people that describe themselves as Geeks are people who are very intelligent. While geeks tend to excel at subjects other people can't comprehend, they tend to fail at figuring out how to make a difference in the world.

Geeks and the world they made

One of the inspirations for this book, came from reading a book about a man named Leonardo de Pisa by Keith Devlin called *Man of Numbers*. Most people would not recognize the name Leonardo de Pisa. This is really too bad, because he was probably one of the most influential and important people in human history. If you don't recognize his real name, you might recognize his nickname, Fibonacci.

Fibonacci's legacy, as revealed in "Man of Numbers", is particularly fascinating because his impact was so significant that it is not obvious to the modern mind. It also doesn't help that the history of his most significant work was virtually forgotten midway through the 20th century, when historians discovered some manuscripts that had sat unread for hundreds of years. These helped piece together Fibonacci's story and come to realize what he had accomplished.

What was Fibonacci's great contribution to humanity? It had nothing to do with the Fibonacci sequence, which is an important never ending sequence of numbers that pops up in surprising places throughout the physical world, from flowers to seashells. It turns out that the Fibonacci sequence was not even discovered by Fibonacci. He simply mentioned it as an example problem in one of his texts on mathematics. Fibonacci's great contribution is also *not* directly related to his mathematical genius, although he was probably the best mathematician in the world during his time.

Fibonacci's great contribution, which changed everything we

know, was *the first math text book*. He was the first mathematician to create a text that was intended to help non-mathematicians learn mathematics. It is this simple text book that fundamentally changed the world and ultimately started us on the path to the technological wonderland we live in today. It could be argued that it was a major contributing factor to the enlightenment a few hundred years later.

It's hard for us to appreciate today, but there was a time when the methods and knowledge of how to solve mathematical problems were strictly limited to mathematical geniuses, and guilds of human computers. These human computers were a vital part of all business transactions in 12th century Vienna, where Fibonacci lived. Fibonacci's math text book was a radical disruption to business at the time, because it eliminated the need for the guild of computers. Instead, common merchants and traders could work out their own business calculations all by themselves. What's more, Fibonacci's text book promoted the easy-to-use Arabic number system because it made calculation easy. Until that time, business transactions performed by computers were calculated using roman numerals on parchment or a highly complex and practiced system of hand gestures, something akin to sign language for arithmetic. The new Arabic system even allowed fancy operations like multiplication and division to be easily performed.

This is not to say there were no texts devoted to mathematics before Leonardo's work. It was common for great mathematicians to compile great tomes intended to demonstrate their wisdom and pass it on to a new generation of mathematicians. But these were math books written by mathematicians for mathematicians. What was truly revolutionary about Leonardo's book was that it was not written for mathematicians, but for ordinary people. People who had previously no ability to perform any sort of mathematical calculations were suddenly learning how to do them on their own.

The guild of specially trained human computers was not thrilled about this revolutionary new text book. It made their services irrelevant. There is historical evidence that the guild made considerable efforts to ban the text book in Vienna, but it was too late. Like a mathematical Prometheus, Fibonacci had stolen the esoteric knowledge of arithmetic from the guild and given it to the common people. In the decades after his death, Fibonacci's content and style of text book was copied by dozens of different authors.

This is one reason why Fibonacci, Leonardo de Pisa, was nearly forgotten by history. His contribution was so widely copied and dispersed that it became difficult to trace back to its origins. In the century after his death, math text books were common. In the century before, they didn't exist.

Man of Numbers describes this, quite rightfully, as the first Information Revolution. We are often aware of the impact the popularization of the internet has had on the world, by providing widespread access to information. Leonardo's contribution to history popularized mathematics, taking from the elite hands of a few, and delivering it into the hands of the masses. Without it, not only would our technology never have been developed, but the volume of everyday commerce that goes on around us without a second thought would have never been possible.

I think this story nicely encapsulates why it's important for geeks to communicate well. It's tempting to believe that our direct and independent actions will make a difference the world. But this is naïve. There are only so many hours in the day, and the human life span is only so long. We can only achieve a finite and relatively small amount on our own. But what can allow someone to make a difference in the world is the sharing of ideas and knowledge. This ability to share what's in our heads acts as a multiplier on what we can achieve in our own lives. Even small ideas can have a huge impact on the world, if they are communicated effectively. Since geeks tend to have a lot of ideas (generally good ones), it makes sense we'd want them to be able to share their insights as widely as possible through proper communication.

In his book, "*The Tipping Point*" Malcolm Gladwell explores how the power of communication can enable a relatively small number or even a single person to radically change the world we live in. He suggests that large scale changes in human culture rarely happen in slow and obvious steps. Instead he suggests that most change comes in sudden and wide sweeping changes that are the result of epidemics of "contagious" ideas. The tale of Fibonacci's impact on the world in *Man of Numbers* is a perfect illustration of this idea. Gladwell suggests that one key fact that determines if an idea is passed on to start an epidemic or if it dies away is its "stickiness". This is used to describe how understandable, memorable and important the idea is perceived to be. But stickiness is not just a property of the idea itself. An idea that is communicated poorly will be perceived as being none of these things. The ability to communicate an idea effectively is a crucial element to make it "sticky".

How did I get in to this?

It might be helpful to explain how I ended up writing a book on communication. It is certainly not, what I would have expected to find myself doing. My background is in software development. Most of my career has been spent as a programmer or a database administrator. I've never had any formal education in communicating. I certainly would not describe myself as someone who is naturally inclined to a role communicating with others. Like many geeks, I'm slightly introverted. Most of the time in my youth was being spent developing technical skills, rather than studying the art of communication through socializing.

Yet since I am not a natural to cover this topic, I can potentially offer some unique insights. As someone who was not inclined to be a natural communicator, I can, with some certainty, say I've had the opportunity to build up a lot of experience on the topic. Most of this experience stems from a few years back, when I had the opportunity to participate in a small high tech start-up. I was originally part of a small group of software developers working on an exciting new technology for databases. Unfortunately, selling this technology was going to be a significant challenge. High tech start-ups are highly risky endeavors to start with, and ours had a serious challenge.

Databases are critical parts of most businesses, the crown jewels of the IT department. Our technology was very complex and very cutting edge. It was complex enough that only the very brightest software developers in our group really understood it at a detailed level. Explaining the technology behind our new product to a potential customer, and convincing them to risk trying it was going to be an extremely difficult challenge. I had the good (or bad) luck to be picked for the role.

This turned out to be a wonderful opportunity for exploring the subject of effective communication. In short, our first attempts to pitch a product built on our technology were a dismal failure. We struggled to get our first few sales because we couldn't explain the value of our product or how it worked without confusing some prospects and scaring others. And then after a few years of improving our sales pitch and explanation of the technology, it became a tremendous success. Our challenge was no longer convincing potential customers that what we had was valuable. Instead it was more mundane things, like getting our software to work perfectly.

There are a few reasons why this turned out to be a perfect scenario to explore how to communicate well. The first is that over a course of 5 years, we were essentially trying to communicate the same message, "Try our product." This provided a wonderful opportunity to make changes to how we delivered that message and study the results. The second is that we were always pitching this message to new potential customers, providing fresh audiences to experiment with. The third reason is the wonderfully objective nature of sales. At the end of the pitch, you either make a sale, or you don't. This gives a very clear gauge of how effective the message was at influencing someone.

Another reason why this was such a fantastic opportunity was that when I started out, I really didn't know what I was doing. As I've said, I am not an expert on communication by any stretch of the imagination, and I'm really not naturally inclined to it. This is a blessing as well as a curse. I've been able to examine and document how I've overcome communication problems because I've been lucky enough to have communication problems to overcome.

I'm also lucky to have a background in programming. This allowed me to approach a conversation like it was a piece of software, debugging the code each time it was run, and then coming up with a new version. During this process I was fortunate enough to be mentored by some extremely effective communicators who were leading our start-up. I was also partnered with an extremely gifted veteran sales person. Following each sales pitch, we reviewed how the interaction with the customer went, and then identified possible ways to improve the delivery of our message. Through this long and repetitive process, we eventually evolved our message from something that was unproductive, to something that was highly effective. Sometimes we made large changes, and sometime we made the slightest tweak. But we always reviewed, and treated each presentation as an opportunity to improve.

Inform or Influence?

I should mention, changing roles was not something I did entirely willingly. To be honest, like many geeks, I found the idea of being "in sales" distasteful. Years later I realize I was not alone. If you are like most people, when I say the words "Sales Person", you are likely to immediately think of some very negative adjectives. Daniel Pink explores this negative connotation in his book "To sell is human." In researching his book, he performed a survey to study how most people perceived the sales profession. He asked people to think of the first word they thought of when they thought of "Sales people". The results were overwhelmingly negative. Of the 25 most common words from the responses, 20 were negative (including "slimy" and "yuck"), whereas only 5 were positive (*if you count words like "challenging" and "necessary" as positive*).

Some geeks might shy away from influencing people because it carries a certain connotation, like sales, that they are uncomfortable with. "Pitching an idea" or "selling it" are not activities most geeks want to find themselves doing. Influencing people is only a short step away from "manipulating" people. It suggests you are actively trying to coerce them into believing something that you want them to believe. Something that is subjective, and not necessarily true.

Manipulating people is clearly wrong. Or is it?

In contrast, if I describe effective communication as a way to inform people, it would probably be completely fine with most geeks. *Teaching* is another very positive word that we could use to describe communication. It implies we are (magnanimously) trying to enlighten an audience on a particular topic by relaying to them facts that are objectively true. Like Fibonacci, who set out on a mission to teach the world how to do mathematics.

Both informing and teaching have a much more passive connotation than *influencing*. It implies it's up to the audience to assess the truth of what is being said. A friend of mine, who is an accomplished software developer, put it this way "You should not twittle someone else's bits". To paraphrase, people should figure out what they believe on their own. But I'd suggest the negative and positive connotations to each of these terms, selling, influencing, teaching or informing are illusionary.

Every time you are communicating an idea, unless you are intentionally trying to deceive your audience, you are communicating what you believe. Regardless if your intent was to passively inform or actively influence, to sell an idea or explain a concept, what you are really doing is actively trying to manipulate your audience into acquiring your ideas.

These ideas originate from millions of neural connections in your brain. When you are communicating with someone, you are actively trying to copy these connections from your brain into the brains of your audience via speech, written symbols or even music and art. When you look at it from this perspective, communication is pretty radical. Effective communication means making *physical changes* in the heads of other people. Even right now, as you are reading this, there are physical effects occurring in your brain. Neural pathways are forming that encode the memory of these words and the ideas they are relaying. There is nothing passive about this.

Here's an example from my own experience. I was once "influenced" (or "manipulated" if you prefer) by my former boss, Albert Lee, during an incident that occurred during our start-up years.

There was a particular customer that was having an issue with our software. They insisted we send someone on site to help them with their issue, and it appeared that someone would be me. I was highly resistant to this idea; there was nothing I could really to do to help this customer, and I didn't want to leave home to fly down to the customer's site. My wife was not happy with all the time I was spending on the road. And besides pulling me off of other valuable technical work, it would cost our cash-strapped start-up a few thousand dollars.

I went into my boss's office, Albert Lee, armed with a set of solid rational reasons why the trip did not make sense. But Albert is an extremely intelligent and insightful man and I now suspect he knew me better than I'd had guessed. He thoughtfully listened to my reasons against the trip. Then he said "Yes, it's true. There will probably not be any technical progress we can make with this trip. *This is a diplomatic mission.*"

Bang! In one sentence, he hooked me. He had taken a cord from one part of my brain, and plugged it into another part, making a connection for me that I had missed. *Of course*, we should demonstrate to the customer that we value them, and are there to support them. *Of course*, I believed in diplomacy. And so I couldn't say no, because I *agreed* with him.

What's fascinating to me then, as is now, was that I knew instantly I'd been hooked with that single sentence, and I was simultaneously completely aware of how I'd been hooked. Albert knew exactly the right words to push my buttons (a direct quote from Star Wars, Episode IV) to make me hear his message and realize the value of the trip. Had he said the same thing using slight different words, I may have stuck to my position and not gone. As Albert was quite a movie buff and I was a geek who grew up with the Star Wars franchise, I was highly suspicious this choice of words was carefully calculated.

The question is was this manipulation? Or was it just being extremely effective at making a point? I'd suggest the only sensible position is that the two are actually the same thing. I walked into his office with one point of view, and begrudgingly walked out with the opposite.

So I challenge geeks to question what they are doing when they are talking to people. Even when we want to be passive communicators, we are actively trying to influence. Even the most innocuous exchange of information has some impact on two people. If there is value and truth in what we are saying, then it should have an influence on people. And if this is the case, then geeks should not shy away from trying to communicate as effectively as possible. Communication is a tool, and like all tools, it can be used for good causes or bad.

I'm not trying to dismiss the good reasons people might associate some styles of communication (typical of some professions like salespeople, politicians and others that make their living convincing people) with a negative stigma. When someone is expressively focused on influencing you (E.g. for example "hard selling") it can be very uncomfortable. There are also some ethical lines that should not be crossed, that do get crossed, either mistakenly or intentionally. Politicians tell lies. Salespeople overstate how great their products are. In general, these ethical lines are drawn along the separation from what is arguably true, and what is obviously false. When these transgressions do occur, and someone is caught saying something that is obviously not true, the entire process of trying to influence people is stuck with a negative image or stereotype. But making this distinction between what is true and not true, especially for topics Geeks like to talk about, is not always as simple as you might assume. We'll explore this topic in greater depth later on in chapter 15 and 16 of this book.

I believe that at least some of the negative connotations attached to the idea of communicating with the intention of influencing also come simply from the insecurities it can arouse in those people that feel they can't do it. It's usually intimidating to confront someone who excels in an ability that you might lack. As we'll discuss in Chapter 2, many geeks are introverts, and naturally shy away from roles where they need to influence other people. Some are extroverts, and actually drive people away from listening to them. We'll examine how these and other common traits of geeks present challenges to communicating effectively.

In Chapter 3, we'll also examine why learning to communicate is a core skill that almost every geek out there should care about. Some people might not immediately see how their communication skills impacts their daily lives. This is because we tend to associate communication with public speaking or perhaps with writing. But effective communication skills come into play in lots of different mediums beyond these obvious ones. There is an array of ways people communicate today. If you are trying to get a message to someone, it's communicating, regardless of if you are addressing them directly, through writing, or in much more subtle ways, like posting a traffic sign, writing a recipe for meat loaf, or adding error messages in a computer program.

Another possible reason sales people might face a negative stigma is since they clearly have an objective in most conversations (E.g. they want to convince you to buy something). This is hardly a fair criticism however. Every time someone, regardless of how passive they are, tries to communicate with someone else, there's an objective at work. In fact, most experts on effective communication will tell you that **objective** is one of the most important concepts in effective communication. Simply put, this is the point of the conversation, the essence of the message you are trying to convey, or the information you are trying to obtain. There is always an objective in a conversation. In fact, when we discuss the topic of objectives in Chapter 10, we'll see there are always multiple objectives in a conversation that need to be recognized and managed. And in Chapter 11, we'll discuss how those objectives can be lost in the noise of a conversation.

Communication is not always easy and it's not always obvious why this is the case. It turns out there is a lot going on in our heads when we try to communicate with one another. In chapter 4 and 5, we'll take a high-level look inside the brain to see what's going on when we speak to each other. We'll touch on all the things that need to happen in order to communicate an idea and some of the interesting and irrational things our brains do that can get in our way.

Effective communication skills also come into play when you are on the other side of the equation. In fact, the first step in being able to communicate your own ideas effectively, as we'll see in chapter 6, is to understand who we are trying to communicate with. In this chapter we'll discuss the concept of *audience*, who it is we are trying to deliver a message to, and why understanding the audience is absolutely critical.

It's my belief that if I can learn to communicate effectively, anyone can learn to communicate effectively. The first challenge is realizing that most of us are not nearly as effective at communicating our ideas as we'd like to be. When you are trying to explain something to someone, and they are struggling to understand, it's very easy to put the blame on the other person. But communication is a two-way interaction. It requires both the speaker and the listener to make an effort to communicate effectively.

This is a communication book written specifically for Geeks, so it will explore communication problems that are specific to geeks. We'll start with technical challenges, like channel capacity in Chapter 7, and move on to deeper challenges, like attitude, in chapter 13.

In most of this book, I'll use the term *audience* and *speaker* to describe the dynamics of communicating. The audience is normally the person or group of people that you are trying to communicate with. In the discussions in this book, the speaker would normally correspond to you, the reader; a person who is trying to communicate with another. There's one danger in using these terms, though. They imply a single direction to communication that is simply not accurate. The roles of audience and speaker often flip in a conversation. Sometimes to make a point effectively, a speaker needs to stop speaking and listen carefully to their audience. And often a speaker may find themselves in the role of questioner, trying to solicit information from their audience. Since effective communication is as much about listening as it is speaking, sometimes we'll view discussions from the other side - as part of someone else's audience. In these discussions, I'll use the term *listener* to correspond to you, the reader. I'll also use these terms, even when discussing written forms of communication, like writing in documents and emails. This is because although the form and dynamics of the conversation are different, the fundamental concepts that are at play in these forms of communication are still the same.

Let's begin by taking a close look at who Geeks are.

Chapter Summary

- The ability to communication effectively is a skill that that everyone needs.
- The goal of all communication is to convey a message to an audience.
- If you want to influence your environment, society and the world, focus on communicating your ideas clearly and effectively.
- Technology made by geeks is rapidly changing the world, but the influence of geeks is not keeping pace.
- Some geeks might be uncomfortable with viewing themselves as actively influencing people, but that is the real goal of all communication.

Chapter 2: Roads less travelled

Here's another handy definition to tell if you might be a geek or not. Geeks are people that are interested in things most people are not. Google provides a less favorable definition than Wikipedia, of who a geek is:

Geek: informal, noun – 1. *An unfashionable or socially inept person.*

Ouch! This definition is clearly less flattering, but *unfashionable* is a very apt term. It's tremendously unfortunate, but science and technology, subjects that geeks are typically interested in, are obvious examples of things that are not particularly fashionable to most people. Mathematics is another clear one. An appreciation of science fiction usually goes along with an interest in science, and I've been told on occasion that it's not cool either. Certainly, not all Geeks are going to be interested in these specific things though. As Wikipedia suggests, you might be a geek if you have a deep interest in just about any subject or hobby. You might be a crochet and knitting geek, or a high altitude kite geek. The key element to being a geek is that mainstream culture doesn't consider the subject or the level of interest in the subject you like popular, fashionable or normal.

There are two potential challenges in communicating effectively that pop-up immediately from being a geek. The first and probably most obvious challenge is that when you're interested in something that no one else is, you're going to find it really hard to find someone to relate to. And when you do try and talk about your interest, you're bound to encounter some resistance. Lots of geeks like science, so let's use it as an example.

Why do some people like something, like science and technology, and others don't? Obviously, there will never be a single answer for that question. But it's probably safe to say that, in some cases, science isn't a popular subject because it can be difficult to understand and many people struggle with it in school as children. Some point to the "boring" way in which science is presented to children[2]. Some blame the way science is separated out as a subject from other subjects, like history or social studies, which makes it seem irrelevant. Some point out that science is portrayed as analytical and cold in contrast to more "lively" subjects like art.

There are also probably biases against these subjects that stem from gender roles that our children are exposed to. In spite of decades of programs to try and interest girls to follow a career in technology and engineering, there remains a significant gender gap in many fields where the number of women is significantly less than the number of men. There is constant debate and theories proposed to explain this lack of interest, none of which I believe are completely compelling. This is a question that is both vital to address, and yet unanswered.

There are also some unfortunate signs that interest in science is actually dropping in both boys and girls in general. An Angus Reid Vision Critical survey of teens in 2012 found that 37% teens aged 16 to 18 were interested in taking a science course after high school, even though 82% of the teens surveyed recognized that studying science would open career opportunities, and 84% of teens believed if fewer people studied science it would negatively impact society. This is an interesting result. Teens today know science is important; it's just that they don't care to do it themselves. They want someone else to do it for them.

Occasionally you will meet a person whose distaste for science goes beyond lack of interest, and has open hostility to the subject and those that represent it. This might be because they are angry about specific or general problems in the world and blame science. Many religious groups see science as a threat to their beliefs, and try to portray it in a negative light. It's very easy to convince people to hate something when they don't understand it.

So if a geek wants to have a conversation with someone about science, there is a distinct risk that they will have some stiff serious trouble. The response from the general populace will be apathy with

---

[2] I for one, like many of my geek friends, never found science boring. Consequently, I don't buy this explanation.

the occasional touch of hostility. And this is, of course, not just limited to science. Every unfashionable subject, from science to knitting to high altitude kite flying will potentially face some of these issues. So the first step to overcoming this challenge is to acknowledge it. Not everyone will be interested in what you are interested in.

If you are lucky enough to find someone that is not as interested in a subject you love, but are willing to engage with you in a conversation about it, you should not take it for granted. I use the word "engage with" specifically in contrast to "listen to" because listening means the other party is not genuinely participating in the conversation. As we'll see in Chapter 7 when we discuss the concept of the channel capacity, it's critical for both sides in a conversation to participate to make the conversation work. It's also important to recognize that your conversational partner may have limited tolerance for a particular subject, both within a single conversation, or a series of conversations. If you have a conversation about astronomy with your significant other on Monday, you may need to skip talking about it on Tuesday, or you will become redundant.

Once you're past the challenge of *topic*, the second challenge many geeks need to face in communicating effectively has to do with the temperments of geeks themselves. This is being an introvert, or (strangely enough) an extrovert. Taken to extremes, both of these personality types can limit one's ability to communicate effectively.

The introverted geek

It's probably not hard to see how being an introvert might lead to underdeveloped communication skills. Many introverts (but not all) are shy. Many introverts find interacting with others tiring, and might be less inclined to pursue situations where they need to communicate effectively. Being a geek introvert possibly makes this harder, however, because Geeks, by definition, are people that might start out with less in common with the average person.

As an adult, having different interests than most people is usually not a significant problem. Adults are usually less concerned about conforming to social expectations. Adults with interests that are uncommon might be hard pressed to find anyone to share them with, but at least they can enjoy them on their own. Children who have different interests can have a tougher time. Children tend to be less accepting and more threatened by others they can't relate to. A child who tries to share a unique interest (for example, science) with his or her peers might risk being ostracized by the peer group because it might feel threatened by something it doesn't understand. Similarly a child who doesn't share the common interests of the peer group (say sports) is also likely to be an outcast. Unlike adults, a child can feel much more pressure to conform to social norms. Most people are still developing a sense of self throughout their childhood and feel insecurity and the need for acceptance more strongly. Young school aged children also typically interact with other children in a social way more than adults whose day is mostly taken up by work.

Psychologists now suspect there might be many possible paths to becoming an introvert. In fact some people might be born introverted to some degree. Studies suggest up to 50% of the traits that are related to introversion may be inherited. But it's also very plausible that children who are less likely to be accepted by their peers might grow up as introverts, and as introverts they might be both less confident in social situations. Since communicating with others is a social skill, it's natural that geeks who are introverts might feel less confident, or less inclined to place importance on communication skills.

Some studies have suggested that introverts make up about 60% of the "gifted" population of children (children that are considered exceptionally bright) but only about 25-40% of the general population[3]. This would possibly result in a feedback mechanism. Children that are introverted are more likely to be misunderstood because they are introverted. That might result in more socialization challenges, which might then make them even more introverted.

So introverts might be weak communicators (or at least feel like ~~they are) because they are less~~ likely to be motivated into

[3] http://giftedkids.about.com/od/glossary/g/introvert.htm

communicating in some situations. They are less likely to speak up in a team meeting, for example, or to voice an opinion when it means taking on some personal risk. This is tremendously unfortunate because it means that there are many situations in today's team-oriented work place that are not conducive to making it easy for introverts to speak out. The solution to this problem is a difficult one. It requires the realization, on the part of the introvert that they have something of value to say, and it should be said. But speaking out (verbally) in a group will always be awkward for an introvert. Many studies have shown that introverts have a hard time in group discussions because they tend to respond slower than extroverts. They seem to devote more time to thinking about how to say what they are going to say, and may generally express less certainty in what they are saying. So managers of introverts need to make an effort to ensure they provide balanced ways for both extroverts and introverts to provide input. For example, it may be better for introverts to communicate in an alternate form of medium, like writing. In contrast to speaking, most introverts have no issues at all writing what they want to say.

    What's interesting is that there is actually active debate about what an "introvert" is in the psychology community. It would be incorrect to assume, for example, that all introverts are shy, although there are clearly some that are. In fact, it's quite the opposite, there are some introverts (like Bill Gates and Warren Buffet) who are very confident in dealing with other people, simply because they don't care about anyone else's opinion. Both shy and confident introverts can suffer from the same communication challenge. Shy introverts might be less inclined to try and communicate, and confident introverts might not care to. Introverts do have one clear advantage when it comes to communicating effectively. They tend to be very effective listeners. In Chapter 8, we'll see how essential this skill is to effectively communicate a message to a specific audience.

    Extroverts and Introverts may also have other differences in their brains. If you are an introvert, you may have experienced the frustration of being in a conversation, and drawing a complete blank when it comes time to say something. Then, hours after the conversation, you think of the perfect comment or witticism. Meanwhile, extroverts seem to be able to ramble on without any problem keeping up. It turns out there may actually be speed differences in the language centers of the brains of introverts and extroverts that account for this difference. As we mentioned in the last chapter, this is why introverts may do better with some forms of communication that are slower, like writing, than fast paced conversations.

However, knowing this is the case; introverts can take several steps to prepare themselves for fast conversations. The prepared list of topics with lead-in lines from the last chapter is one example. This works well because it removes the time aspect from the process completely. Similarly, if introverts are planning on having a conversation where they'll need to deal with questions, they can improve their ability to respond by imagining what the questions are ahead of time, and then practicing answers. When the time comes to deal with the question in a conversation, they can pull the answer from memory, rather than having to reason it out on their feet.

Besides speed, studies have found that introverts may have less capacity for short term memory, but a higher capacity for long term memory. A higher capacity for long term memory has some obvious benefits, particularly for the recognition of underlying patterns in events. But short term memory is particularly important for casual conversations. It helps track minor details, like a person's name, that are not critical to overall understanding of a conversation, but that are nonetheless important to the mechanics of moving the conversation along.

I've noticed this of myself. I consider myself to be socially intuitive. I have no trouble picking up subtle signs of people's moods. And in conversations I can easily identify the main concerns a person has. But I also find I struggle a great deal to retain simple facts, like people's names, or where they are from. This can lead to some pretty awkward situations. I often run into people I've had deep discussions with and I remember everything about the challenges and direction in their IT environment, but I can't remember what their name is. It just didn't register in my brain as something that should be retained. I've learned to compensate for my poor short term memory by discretely taking notes to retain the information my brain is not inclined to; I jot down people's names and roles, and sometimes some personal information about them, if they share any. I rarely need to refer to these notes. The simple act of writing these things down is usually enough to trigger the brain to retain the information.

This sort of weakness in casual conversation can be a real challenge for introverts in the business world. Making small talk is, on occasion, an important skill to have in order to gain influence with people. It's an activity where extroverts do very well. If you think of the stereotype of an executive schmoozing with clients out on the golf course, it's easy to see that the ability to make small talk can play a large role in business. I would dread being stuck on a golf course, not just because of my poor golf skills, but also because of the obligation to make small talk during the entire game.

I don't want to suggest that all geeks are introverts however. There are some geeks, albeit fewer, that are undoubtedly extroverts. When you meet them, they are hard to miss. These geeks seem to have reacted in the opposite way to having different interests. Instead of turning inward and becoming quieter people, they have turned up the volume. These are the geeks that revel in flaunting their uniqueness; the ones that love talking as much as possible.

The extroverted geek

Ironically, being an extreme extrovert also leads to a serious communication challenge. They don't suffer from the same inhibition against speaking up that introverts do, but instead they tend to be very bad listeners. Many extroverts don't pick up on the fact when they've completely lost the understanding or interest of their audience. They can miss the subtle clues that indicate someone has grown tired of them talking, or that it's time for the flow of conversation to reverse to give someone else a chance to talk. Conversations with an extroverted geek can be frustrating because they tend to overpower everyone else.

Of being too introverted or too extroverted, I'd suggest that being too extroverted is in fact more of a challenge. The social implications are different. An introverted geek may be prone to being ignored in a social setting. An extroverted geek may be actively shut out by his or her social group because they are perceived as overbearing and annoying. I'd suggest it's also easier to overcome introversion than extroversion. Besides building up the courage to speak out more often, it is possible for introverts to be heard via writing. However, I believe the best cure for too much extroversion is much harder. It requires developing personal discipline to avoid overpowering other people in conversations. Extremely extroverted geeks need to make a constant attempt to tone down their excitement about a subject and allow others to occasionally speak too. We'll return to this point again later, but it is essential that conversations have a back and forth flow, where both parties are allowed to give input. For an extrovert, this is not necessarily an easy task.

Finally, I suspect extroversion is a harder challenge to overcome, because if you are an extroverted geek, it's highly likely no one will tell you about it for a couple reasons. First, you might be surrounded by introverts that are too quiet to tell you. Second, unlike introversion, extroversion is not perceived as a personality trait problem. As Susan Cain points out in her book on Introverts, "Quiet", if you are introverted, it will likely be pointed out to you many times in your life. You will be constantly encouraged to "Come out of your shell". Extroversion is more socially acceptable, *but extreme extroversion is not*. When someone is too extroverted, people say he or she is loud and annoying. The blame is placed on the person, rather than the personality trait. No one says that an extrovert should "Get more into his shell".

Geeks as a social group

Whether you are a geek who is an introvert or extrovert, there is usually no denying that being a geek (at least in the current era) usually comes with some feelings of marginalization and separation from the rest of society. The fact that we have the word "geek" illustrates this separation is real. Popular culture (and geek culture, if there is such a thing) is constantly evolving though, so this might not always be the case.

I'm a fan of the TV show "Big Bang Theory". The high ratings of this show indicate a very large number of other people are as well. Regardless of if you enjoy it or hate it, you can't deny the fact that the show is highly popular. You might not think that a show about nerdy physicists and engineers and their hot neighbor would have mass appeal. But this show is relevant to two large groups of people. There are all the geeks that identify with the main characters. There are also all the people who know the geeks and relate them to the show's main characters (they probably identify themselves with Penny - the lone non-geek on the show). Combined, these two groups of TV audiences make a very large market.

This is significant because comedy is usually an excellent bellwether for social forces. For something to be humorous, it needs to be relevant and somehow insightful. We usually find things funny "because they're so true". For a TV comedy to be successful, it needs to be funny to a large number of people. "Big Bang Theory" is funny to a wide audience because it's relevant to a wide audience.

Most of the comedy on Big Bang is centered on the four main characters who, as geeks, struggle with social ineptitude and finding acceptance in a society that does not understand them. This is, of course, a stereotype, or at least a caricature. Not all geeks are socially inept. Not all geeks are shy. But there is also no denying that there is at least some truth to the stereotype that many geeks are less socially adept, this is why the show is funny.

I think that so many people find the show funny is a good indication of where geeks stand in society today. Twenty years ago, it's highly unlikely that "The Big Bang Theory" would have been a hit show, or even be on television at all, because geeks were not "main stream". No one would have really appreciated the show. But without a doubt, Geeks are now on the radar of mainstream culture. The conflict for acceptance between the characters and society in the show mirrors a conflict for acceptance between geeks everywhere and society. The reason geeks are on the radar of pop culture is, without a doubt, all the high-tech goodies made by geeky people that the world is so hungry for. Geeks have come along for the ride, and now society at large is trying to make sense of them. This is a golden opportunity then, for

Geeks everywhere to seize, if they just learn how to grasp it. Geeks have found a place on the world stage, so to speak, and now we just need to work out what we want to say (and how to say it).

Chapter Summary

- Geeks are often interested in things that are not popular, which can present a communication challenge.
- If you are talking to someone who is less interested in a topic you like, but is still willing to speak about it, don't take it for granted by going on too long, or repeating the same subject the next time you talk.
- Introverted geeks may be less inclined to speak out. They need to realize that what they have to say is valuable, and beneficial to others around them.
- Managers of introverts need to make efforts to provide ways for both extroverts and introverts to provide input.
- Introverts might feel more comfortable communicating through writing, rather than through speaking.
- Extroverted geeks can easily overpower and annoy others in a conversation.
- Extroverted geeks must develop the personal discipline to listen to, rather than overpower others in a conversation.

Chapter 3: Why should communication matter to Geeks?

We've discussed why geeks, both introverted and extroverted, might have weaknesses in their communication skills. Next we'll address the question of why communication skills matter so much. After all, why should Geeks devote themselves to building better communication skills to bridge the gap between geeks and non-geeks? I think anyone would agree that science, technology, and mathematics are typical geek interests that are very important to the world. Effective communication is essential for geeks because they are interested in fields that have great influence and that continue to grow.

Geeks at work – In Science

To explore this idea, let's look at two professions where we would expect to find geeks. Geeks tend to like science and engineering. Examining jobs in these fields might provide some insight on how reliant geeks are on their communication skills to make a living.

Isaac Newton famously said "If I have seen further, it is because I stood on the shoulders of Giants." For someone who achieved so much in the field of science, his words may be taken as a statement of exemplary modesty. But I believe that he is simply stating the facts.

Newton undeniably provided us with the first sensible account of how bodies move (Newton's laws of motion), why we don't float away into the sky (Newton's Law of Gravitation), and how many squares you can fit under a funny curve (calculus). None of these advancements would have been possible without the ground work laid by centuries of previous scientists, philosophers and mathematicians. Before becoming the father of physics, Isaac Newton was a student like any other person, studying books of other great minds. And even after he became the father of physics, he still continued to learn a great deal from other great minds of the day. Most of what we know about Isaac and his work comes from letters corresponding with others.

If you do happen to work as a scientist, or in a scientific related field, this is obvious. Scientists spend a significant amount of their time as writers, describing in detail what they did, how they did it, and why. Scientific communities revolve around their core scientific journals. These provide scientists a way to share observations and theories with other scientists, so new work can be reviewed, criticized, and accepted or rejected.

Like most human beings, scientists like to eat and buy things. Having a building for work is also a nice advantage. For most scientists, that means securing funding for their work from a university, government or business. This is as close to a pure sales job as one can get. If a scientist cannot convince anyone of the value of their work, he or she will not stay a scientist for long.

Effective communication skills are critical to scientists. Without the ability to make a convincing sales pitch for their work, scientists will be unable to secure funding. Without the ability to clearly explain and document their work, scientists would be unable to share their insights with each other.

Scientists also sometimes bear an enormous burden of responsibility to shepherd the application of their work. Albert Einstein is famous for his work on physics, some of which ultimately lead to the development of atomic weapons. Realizing the danger of such weapons, he devoted much of his later life to the peace movement, to prevent the use of such weapons. Similarly, Robert Oppenheimer, "Father of the atomic bomb" risked (and lost) his career and public life campaigning against a nuclear arms race and proliferation of the devastating weapons. Both men recognized the dire impact their work could have on the world if it was used irresponsibly. It was their ability to communicate that enabled them to act on this realization, and convince others that a war involving nuclear weapons would be a risk too horrific and damaging for humanity.

The act of communicating is essential to the progress of

science. What is perhaps most intriguing about the case of Isaac Newton is that while Isaac Newton had developed one form of calculus in England, another great mind, Gottfried Wilhelm Leibniz, had independently developed an equivalent form in Germany. You might say that Newton invented derivatives, and Leibniz invented integrals (the inverse operation of derivatives). Calculus was a tremendous advance for humanity. That two people would stumble on it at the same time is seemingly miraculous at first.

It's certainly not without precedent though. History is littered with these seemingly unlikely and coincidental developments of major breakthroughs that pop up in multiple places from multiple people at the same time. These coincidences have often resulted in bitter disputes about who got there first.

What I find fascinating about these occurrences is that it suggests that perhaps who got there first is actually not that important, because they are not coming from these great minds, as much as through them. Consider that Isaac Newton and Gottfried Wilhelm Leibniz both drew their ideas from a set of common data and previous knowledge, made available through the exchange of information between great minds of the 17th and 18th century. They both worked on solving the same mathematical and scientific problems of the day, and both came up with equivalent (if inverse) solutions. So their great work was perhaps the result of a set of convergent ideas.

If great works like calculus, electricity, the light bulb or the telephone are convergent, then maybe it's really the whole of society that deserves the credit. Maybe when the world is ready to realize some idea, it can pop up in several places at once. To be clear, I would not claim ownership of the ideas expressed in this book. They are the result of lessons and ideas I inherited from a variety of sources. They've come through mentors I have learned from, books I have read, and speakers that have influenced me. My contribution is to combine these ideas from various sources in this book to make them relevant to a particular topic, in the same tradition as Fibonacci (who, you recall, did not discover the Fibonacci sequence, but did document it in his math text book).

If this is the case, then a key criterion for promoting scientific progress is establishing free lines of communication between scientists, and encouraging them to pursue every opportunity to improve their communication skills. This would ensure that ideas could flow easily to the great minds of our day, and then be realized. Isaac Newton went on to say, "The success of others put me upon considering it; and if I have done anything which may be useful to following writers, I have my design."

Geeks at work – In Engineering

Engineering is another occupation where we're sure to find geeks working. Before we get into too much depth about why engineers might need good communication skills, I'd like you to consider a broader application of the term "engineering", since lots of people work with technology today.

I work in the IT industry, where most of the people I work with are software developers, product managers, or solution architects (people that combine or configure software to solve a particular set of problems). The number of actual engineers is relatively small however, even though we all work in an "engineering" department. And this is pretty typical of most companies today.

There are many other examples of people from other industries, like banking, education, and manufacturing, that are employed to innovate and develop technological solutions to problems. I'd like you to consider that the term *engineering* is the most appropriate term to apply to all of these situations. After all, without a name, how can we effectively discuss this work? What education do people really need to do it, if it's not an education in engineering? How should people approach this activity? Are there any best practices they can use, or pitfalls they should avoid?

Engineering programs at universities are professional degrees, which mean regardless of what college or university you attend, you will likely take a series of courses with similar content. This content is developed by a collaboration of professional engineering associations and the schools to ensure graduates have (in theory) the necessary background they need to do a job in engineering when they are done. And if you take a professional engineering degree at university, you will likely take some form of "communication" course. This will likely be a short, relatively easy course, taken in the first semester of your program. During this course, you will likely be told at some point that the practice of engineering is 90% understanding a problem, and 10% fixing it. The course will typically be considered a "Bird course" by most of the students. It will briefly mention communication skills are important to engineering, and then possibly spend some time teaching specific skills like drafting or even sketching. It is likely the only "art" course most engineers will ever take.

After this short course, most engineering programs will devote half of their time directly to subjects and skills related to their core area of study, and half of their time to a mix of advanced mathematics, physics, chemistry, and other science subjects. I'll tell you a secret that most engineers will readily confirm. It will not shock anyone, except maybe those professors that teach in colleges and universities. In actual practice, the majority of engineers rarely, if ever, use the majority of knowledge directly acquired in these engineering classes. Advanced vector calculus, for example (a corner stone of engineering education), is rarely touched by engineers. Mathematicians might do advanced vector calculus and mathematics software certainly does advanced vector calculus, but engineers do not.

The short "bird courses" on communication, however, are critical and immediately relevant to everyday engineering work. This is because engineering is inherently a social activity. Communication and social skills are vital to engineers performing their duties. Unfortunately, this aspect of engineering education is so neglected and poorly delivered that those without any engineering education perform just as well as those with it.

Engineering as social activity

Most engineers will hear the following story at some point in their education. It involves a luxury high- rise apartment (or sometimes a luxury hotel) in New York (sometimes it's L.A.), where the residents were upset about the time spent waiting for the elevator.

An engineering firm was hired to develop a faster elevator system, so people would not have to wait as long. Unfortunately, every option they looked at for increasing the speed of the elevators was prohibitively expensive. And after studying the current elevator, the firm realized that the elevator was actually quite fast, and the wait time was relatively low.

Finally, one engineer realized the problem they were trying to solve was not to make the elevators go faster, but rather to make the wait more bearable for people waiting for the elevator. The people waiting were frustrated because they were bored, not because the elevator was that slow. Consequently, they had the building install mirrors on the elevator doors. Looking at themselves in the mirror occupied people's attention while they waited for the elevator.

This story has been around the engineering profession for a long time; long enough that it's actually questionable whether it actually happened. It may just be a really great illustration of the core idea behind engineering —the key to a good solution is to understand the definition of the problem. Most discussions about this story stop at this point, but I'd like to go a little deeper. It's tempting to stop, since the conclusion is that you need to understand a problem before you try to solve it is pretty obvious. But it also lacks real insight. You need to understand any problem before solving it. The question is *how do you do that?*

So let's consider, "What skills did the engineer in question need to solve this problem?" Was it an understanding of physics? Or a grasp of elevator mechanics? Those were surely relevant to the task of deciding which solutions would not work. But they didn't contribute at all to the final solution. Instead, the insight that allowed the engineer to solve the problem in this story came from an understanding of human psychology. The key insight was that people were still bored and frustrated waiting for the elevator, even when the elevator was fast.

Let's keep going...How did the engineer in the story make this insight into human psychology to come up with the mirror solution? How can those doing engineering ensure that they understand a problem before they try to solve it? The story doesn't mention this detail, but I think we can safely assume the simplest explanation. The engineer must have realized it, after he or she talked to the residents of the building. Communication is the obvious key to understanding another person's problem. It is not just the ability to put out information, but also to take it in. Engineering, you see, is a highly social activity requiring proficiency in social skills like effective communication.

In fact, I think you would be hard pressed to find a profession with more social interaction. The need for effective communication is not limited to just people trying to solve the problem (engineers and technologists) and people with the problem (labeled as "problem owners" by engineers). Collaborating on a complex piece of technology requires deep interaction between peers, because modern technological systems are simply too big and complex for a single person to understand at a single time. It requires many people to create the next *Angry Birds*, or produce the next *iPad*. Engineers must constantly collaborate with each other to build a working solution.

Most jobs require some peer interaction before or after a task. A teacher might interact with other teachers when planning a day's lesson, or when discussing a student's academic struggles. But when interacting with students, there is a different, more limited form of social interaction. A teacher and a student are not peers, so the types of social interactions between them are much more limited (this is because of a social hierarchy). Unlike a grade school class, people working on technology together do so without a clear social hierarchy that decides who is right and wrong. This requires individuals to balance the demands of their own egos with the demands of the group for mutual respect and fairness.

Modern technology problems are also typically complex with no clear or obvious answer. This requires technologists to be cautious in their vision and opinions. They always need to consider the possibility their opinion might be wrong, requiring a certain detachment from their own ideas, and openness to the ideas of others.

After all, modern technology is, quite literally, built on the ideas of others. Our high-tech world is not just a testament to the human ability to use tools, but the human ability to cooperate and collaborate in groups.

Breaking down Engineering Stereotypes

So why don't we think of engineering as a social activity? Why are engineers pigeon holed as introverts? Why are they, so often, actually introverts? I think the idea of engineering as social activity runs contrary to most stereotypes of engineers, including those held by engineers themselves. There aren't too many reasonable depictions of engineers doing engineering in literature or media. Talking to some of my colleagues, the only one we could come up with was "Scotty" on the TV show Star Trek. There's no doubt that this show has had a huge impact on popular culture, and influenced generations of geeks and other technically minded people.

Many of these people would idealize themselves as a "Scotty" type. Unfortunately, I think very few people actually stop to realize that Scotty, Geordi LeForge and the other "chief engineers" from the Star Trek series are actually the *other* kind of engineer. Their primary job is to keep the engines running on the Starship, or at least fix them in the nick-of-time, usually through unconventional hacking and dramatic heroics.

Besides this Scotty/MacGyver stereotype, there is also a second, more historically based stereotype, which is the "Inventor". This is a much older and ingrained stereotype typified by our idealized picture of historical figures like Alexander Graham Bell, Thomas Edison, Elisha Gray, Nicola Tesla, Isaac Newton and countless others. Simplified stories of these famous inventors are taught to small children, and tend to stick with us our whole lives.

Unfortunately, this "inventor" stereotype also does not fit with the reality of engineering, or how most of these historical figures actually worked. If you pick any one at random, and actually read up on the history of that figure, you'll find that inevitably it's a story with some controversy and conflict around whether it was really them that first stumbled upon their breakthrough (E.g. Bell with the telephone, Edison with the light bulb, Newton with Calculus) - or was it some other contemporary (E.g. Elisha Gray with the telephone, Tesla with the light bulb, Leibniz with Calculus). And it's extremely rare that any of the many people that helped these figures carry out their historical work are noted (Mr. Watson is one obvious exception), but they were undoubtedly there. Our simple caricature histories of these people simply do not fit reality.

I think this is generally true for historical cases because it's unreasonable to picture any of these figures working away on their own. They didn't just tinker away in a small workshop by themselves, as we often like to picture. They employed teams of people working in their labs and workshops. Some of the ideas that contributed to their famous inventions undoubtedly came from other nameless people via social interaction. This gets lost in history because at the end of the day, it's only the boss who has their name on a patent. Edison is famous for having thousands of patents. To believe that he actually came up with all those ideas, all on his own is preposterous. This historical simplification is partially due to the patent system, which was never intended to record the credit for all the people that contributed to an invention, only the *ownership* of the invention.

This knowledge is important because without it our ideas about engineering and how it works would be skewed. Engineering is not an activity done by individuals, but by networks of people working together. It's an inherently social activity.

Like scientific ideas, the emergence of a particular invention might be inevitable. Several groups or individuals might simultaneously realize that next development, not because of their own personal gifts or insights, but because all the precursors for that next step are in place. Exploring if this hypothesis is true is beyond the scope of this book. However, it does have serious implications, for companies that make their business by trying to innovate. Communication needs to be recognised as a core engineering skill and activity, and a prerequisite to innovation.

The nature of the beast

Once while I was working for our start-up, I had a conversation with one of our sales executives, while waiting to meet a mutual customer. The executive was excited at the prospect of out-sourcing some of our software development to India. The incentive for this move was largely to cut the cost of development, while increasing the speed at which they could deliver new software. This struck me as an obviously bad move (which thankfully never did materialize), but I was a little taken aback that it would even be suggested. Our software was cutting edge and extremely complex; an off-shore team would not help development.

To confess, I was not in a great mood during this conversation. I had been swamped all week trying to work around a serious technical short-coming in our product that another customer was upset about. Then I was pulled off it at the last minute, to fly down to New Jersey. The last minute flight was extremely expensive (being a starved start-up, cash is always precious), and the trip would waste two critical work days. Our executives had insisted on it however, since they felt it was critical to meet the customer face-to-face. In spite of the enormous cost of these trips, they felt actually talking to them in person produced better results than online presentations or conference calls. It allowed the customer to engage more freely with us, helped build a deeper and stronger relationship.

This isn't a rare approach to sales. In fact, I don't think you would find anyone in sales that would not prefer to meet their customers face-to-face. There is no question, among sales people, that doing sales is a highly social activity. The deep irony is that engineering and related activities like software development are also highly social activities.

There are, of course, cases where outsourcing to lower paid, remote contractors may work, both for sales and for software development. For example, in sales, telemarketing generally works when you are selling very simple, low cost products to a very large market, and expect a very low success rate for each sales call. The key to success in this type of sales approach is volume, so you want to increase the number of sales people, and pay them as little as possible to reduce the "cost" of a sale.

Of course, you can't sell products that are expensive this way, or products that are very complex, because no one would buy them. The risk to the buyer is much too high. Complex or expensive products require time to consider, and more information than a quick telephone call allows. You also could not sell products with a very small market via telemarketing. A small potential market requires a very high success rate. That means using fewer, but more skilled, sales people.

For software developers, engineers and other technologists, it is exactly the same. Outsourcing works when you have a very large amount of very simple technology problems to solve, that do not require lots of communication. This is not, a situation that comes up a lot. If a technology problem is extremely simple, it's probably already solved. Unlike sales, technical solutions tend to be easily reproducible; they are usually solved once, and then copied. There's not a lot of "Grunt work" in IT. Adding more low-cost people usually does not help. As Warren Buffet once said: "No matter how great the talent or efforts, sometime things just take time. You can't produce a baby in a month by getting nine women pregnant".

In fact, if a technology problem is simple enough to be done without social interaction, there exists the strong possibility that it's simple enough to be done without people at all. It may in fact, be done by other software. In software development, this typically will mean using an existing library or framework that reduces or eliminates the work required to produce a solution. Sometimes it might involve using a code generator to produce more software.

On the other hand, if a problem is complex, it may require hiring a minimal number of programmers, not a maximum. This is a fact that most people doing software development immediately recognize. It has been around for many years, and was probably best communicated in the book *The Mythical Man-Month* in 1980. The issue is fairly simple. Development of a large software program is highly interactive. The task of writing a program is always divided up between different people in a group. Each person will typically work on one part of the program (User interface, database) or one set of tasks (Eg, testing). Each person will typically develop expertise in one area, and rely on others to be experts in the aspects they don't have time to understand. No one can become an expert in everything.

However, as the number of people in the group increases, more time and effort needs to be spent managing and coordinating the group. The efficiency of the group decreases as it grows, and eventually reaches a point where time is being spent just organizing the group, rather than doing actual work. It becomes harder to keep track of who is doing what. It's not clear which member of the team is an expert in a particular area. Personal conflicts and bruised egos are more likely to challenge the smooth functioning of the group as a whole.

Smart software development shops almost always carefully manage the number of people assigned to a project to ensure they do not involve more people than necessary. They understand that cheap labor has absolutely no benefit to tasks like software development. In fact, it's a serious threat to meeting development goals.

Ironically, one of the most gifted "engineers" I've worked with was our Vice-president of Sales, Roger Walker. In all fairness, Roger, *was* an engineer by education, but did not perform a job that would be described as engineering; he was a salesperson. You might assume a role in sales is a far reach from engineering, but they are, in fact, very close. An excellent salesperson is one that takes the time to talk to their customer, and understand their problem[4]. Once he does that, he can position whatever it is he is selling correctly. Or, in some cases, decides that his goods do not fit the customer's need and walks away.

On more than one occasion, Roger was able to evoke the customer's real problem where others had failed to understand it. This allowed our developers to offer a solution to that problem, and satisfy the customer. It's also notable, that of all our executives and sales people, Roger was the one person outside of engineering that all the developers seemed to know. This was possibly because he occasionally

[4] This explains why, aside from ending up in management, professionally trained engineers tend to end up in sales.

brought them bags of candy. But more significantly, it was because he made an effort to interact with them on occasion. I suspect this was intentional and pragmatic. The developers were part of Roger's team, and Roger felt you should know the people on your team. At the same time, he recognized that they had a job to do that was separate from his, and would not constantly pester them in an attempt to micromanage their work, like many business managers attempt to do. This approach was highly effective.

Since science and engineering are both social activities that require strong communication skills, it's critical to look about how that social interaction can be fostered, and how it might be hampered. One obvious way to fail is to ignore the social aspect all together, and assume technologists are commodity resources that can easily be outsourced to the lowest cost supplier on the other side of the world. Both engineers and executives in a business need to look beyond the stereotypes of engineers in pop culture and realize the social nature of engineering activities. Scientists need to recognize that the more they communicate, the more likely they are to make progress.

There is a serious danger of misinterpreting this idea however. In her book *Quiet,* Susan Cain admonishes (quite rightfully) the importance placed on being an extrovert. Susan cites the example of Isaac Newton as a noted introvert, and points out that had he been an extrovert, he might have been much less likely to devote his time and energy to work on gravity and mathematics. *Quiet* explains the dangers of attempting to construct a world based on extrovert ideals. Cain also points out that the popularity of open concept offices is one clear example of how the world we live in is being shaped in the assumption that everyone should be an extrovert. As she explains, a majority of leaders in the business world are extroverts, and are constantly told in institutions like the Harvard School of Business that the secret to success is to be an extrovert. These MBAs then carry that assumption with them into the work places everywhere and try to shape their environment to conform to these ideas of what an effective organization should look like if it was staffed exclusively by extroverts.

Susan points to a large number of studies however that consistently and clearly show "open concept" offices are much *less* productive for organizations, even for organizations like engineering and science that should benefit from a highly social environment. In fact, besides lowering productivity, open concept offices increase stress, sick days, and employee dissatisfaction.

So is this in conflict with the idea that some professions like engineering and science are social activities that should benefit from effective communication?

The answer is absolutely not. As an example, Isaac Newton was noted to be extremely introverted and reclusive. This probably encouraged his passion for math and physics. But his genius was made also possible because of his social interactions via his correspondence with others. He simply favored a different kind of social interaction that was more controlled and slow. I would hate to imagine what would have happened if he had been forced to work in an open-concept office where he had to contend with co-workers.

The fault in the assumption behind open-concept offices is that more social interaction is the same thing as *quality* social interaction – that communicating *a lot* is the same thing as communicating *effectively*, when clearly these are not the same thing. Open concept offices make effective communication much harder because they drown out meaningful communication in noise. They remove barriers that allow introverts to recharge their social batteries, making them less inclined to communicate. It's quantity at the expensive of quality.

Now that we've established that communication is important, let's start to look at how we can do it better.

Chapter Summary

- Science and engineering are both highly social activities. Both scientific and engineering advancements rely on communication and social interaction.
- Like other social activities (E.g. sales) neglecting this social aspect can lead to failure. To help them flourish, companies and organizations should create an environment that encourages communication.
- This does not mean everyone should be an extrovert, or that office environments should be designed to extrovert ideals. It is critical to recognize the difference between high quantity communication and high quality communication.

Chapter 4: How rational is your thinking?

As a geek, one of the biggest challenges I found in becoming a communicator was my faith in the inherent rationality of people. I always believed a rational argument should be a convincing argument.

People can be rational, but their brains are often not. Even you, dear reader, are much less rational then you might assume. To prove it, consider this experiment you can try on yourself, borrowed from Dean Buonomano's excellent book *Brain Bugs - How the brain's flaws shape out our lives*. *Brain Bugs* examines the ways our brains workings sometimes lead us astray. This experiment will require you to make a choice as fast as possible. Below are two sentences that provide you different choices, read the problem as fast as possible, and note which answer you pick.

Assume you are given $50. You are then given a choice:
A) You can KEEP forty nine percent of the money.
B) You can LOSE forty nine percent of the money.

And now read the question more closely. If you are like most people, you would probably pick 'A' as your first choice. It's natural to want to keep the something of value, so your brain automatically hones in on the word keep and makes a positive association with it. Similarly, the word lose has a negative association. So the brain is naturally inclined to pick 'A' as the answer, even though, with some slower and more careful reading, it's obvious that 'B' is actually the preferable answer.

The effect word choices have on how people evaluate value and risk has been very well studied over the years. This question nicely demonstrates how the wording of a simple choice can significantly change the choices people made. This is what's known as 'framing'.

This was so interesting that I had to try it myself. So I sent the following email to a group of friends and family:

Greetings everyone,

*As part of the research for an upcoming book, I'm conducting a little experiment, designed to illustrate how people perceive a **choice**. So I've sent this question to most people I know.*

If you could take a quick second and pick 'A' or 'B' from the two choices below, and email me back your choice, I'd greatly appreciate it. Your choice will be anonymous, and your name won't be used in any way.

*If you know anyone else that received this email, please don't discuss the **question** with them.*

You have $50, and are given a choice.
*A) You can **keep** $30.*
B) You can take a gamble with a 50/50 chance of keeping or losing the full $50.

Then I sent the following email to a second, equally sized group:

Greetings everyone,

*As part of the research for an upcoming book, I'm conducting a little experiment, designed to illustrate how people perceive **risk**, so I've sent this question to most people I know.*

If you could take a quick second and pick 'A' or 'B' from the two choices below, and email me back your choice, I'd greatly appreciate it. Your choice will be anonymous, and your name won't be used in any way.

*If you know anyone else that received this email, please don't discuss the **problem** with them.*

You have $50, and are given a choice.

*A) You can **lose** $20.*
B) Take a gamble with a 50/50 chance of keeping or losing the full $50.
Thanks!

Mathematically, there is no difference between the problems

posed in either email. In both cases, the first choice provided (keep $30 or lose $20) is actually the exactly same. So rationally, we'd expect the breakdown of responses between A and B to be about the same.

The Impact of Framing

The only difference in these messages is the words used to describe the safe choice. In the first, it's posed as "Keeping $30", and in the second "Losing $20". In addition, the email describes the situation in different terms. The first uses the more positive words "choice" and "question", while the second uses the more negative words "risk" and "problem". So what difference did the word choice have in the responses? Clearly, it had some effect, because the people that received the second email with negative wording were much more likely to stick to safe choice A, and keep their imaginary $30.[5]

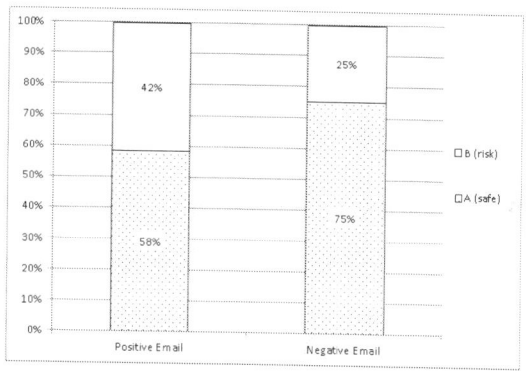

Figure 1 - Survey responses show a clear difference in how the risk was perceived based on the wording of the question.

This particular type of framing is known as 'Loss Aversion'. In short, most of us (some more than others) don't like the idea of losing

---

[5] Also noticeable in the group that received the "negative" email were a noticeable number of responses of people that tried "bargaining" - asking about any other options, or complaining that neither choice was good. Even though the $50 was imaginary, they still didn't want to lose the $20.

something precious and will naturally favor choices that appear to be lower risk. As Dean Buonomano, points out in *Brain Bugs*, the susceptibility to this and other types of framing can result in irrational choices with serious implications. He cites one example of a study by psychologists Kahneman and Tversky that showed doctors' decisions to recommend a medical procedure was heavily influenced by whether the procedure had a 90 percent survival rate, or a 10 percent mortality rate. It showed Doctors would much rather have 90% of their patients survive than have 10% die (even though those are exactly the same).

You can see another type of framing at work every time you go shopping. People love sales that offer discounts of 10, 25 or even 50% off. What a deal! A discount uses framing to trick the brain into believing we're gaining something, even though it really means we're just losing a little less (and that's assuming the regular price wasn't artificially inflated to start with).

Framing isn't just limited to word choices either. Here's another nice example of an optical illusion that exploits framing. Consider the picture on the next page. Which of the circles in the center of each group is larger, the left or right? The answer is actually neither; the two center circles are exactly the same size. It's the presence of the large circles on the left that make the brain more likely to perceive the center circle as smaller, and the presence of the small circles on the right that makes the brain perceive the small circle as large.

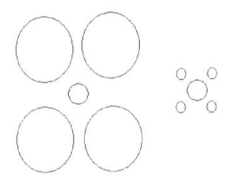

Figure 2- A simple optical illusion - The brain is inclined to see the circle on the left as smaller than the circle on the right, because it's smaller relative to the larger circles surrounding it, while the one on the right is larger than the circles surrounding it. This is a form of framing.

Psychologists have studied framing effects heavily for many decades now. It's important to note that its effects don't work equally for all people or in the same way for all people. Both introverts and extroverts may react differently to negative or positive framing effects. Perhaps some people who are exceptionally logical and methodical in their thinking may be immune to framing effects. But you need to prepare for the likely case that they are not.

I'd suggest, as geeks, we often tend to dismiss the importance of the effect of words. This is because geeks do tend to favor a slower and rational response to messages. This tends to diminish the effects of framing. Unfortunately, if you are trying to reach an audience, you can't assume the audience will react slowly and rationally to what you are saying. They will sometimes follow the tone of words, so you need to be cautious about your word choices and think about how they will influence your audience's reaction. Negative words can trigger fear or loss aversion, while positive words can do the opposite, even when they are used to say the same thing. To combat these effects, or to exploit them, it's good to quantify words as 'Negative' or 'Positive' when reviewing a message. Framing a statement using negative words when you are trying to evoke a positive response usually backfires, just as a negative message does when it's framed in positive terms. By quantifying words, it becomes easier to objectively gauge whether they will have their intended effect on your audience.

For the audience, this also works in reverse. If you want to evaluate a message as rationally as possible, it's sometimes helpful to first translate any strongly positive or negative words into more neutral words to help remove the effects of framing. This "just the facts" approach helps focus on the facts of the message, rather than on the feeling of the message.

Fear

If you recall from the last chapter, we discussed the influence extroversion or introversion could have on how a geek is perceived by the world around them. It turns out whether you are an extrovert or introvert also has implications for how you perceive risk in the world around you. In fact, the differences in how extroverts and introverts perceive risk might explain why introverts can feel as if talking to a stranger at a party might put their life in mortal danger, while an enthusiastic and talkative extrovert can be oblivious to when complete strangers might feel like killing him because he won't stop talking.

It turns out that introverts and extroverts actually perceive risk differently. In the experiment with the $50, it's quite possible that extroverts would be less likely to choose 'A - Keep 49%' than 'B LOSE 49%', not necessarily because they were more rational about their choices, but because they were less adverse to risk to start with. As Susan Cain describes in 'Quiet', physiologist Jerome Kagan, studied this effect in a landmark research project that started in 1989. Kagan started his study looking at 500 four month old babies, examining how they reacted to various stimuli like a popping balloon. The children returned to his lab at two, four and eleven years, gauging further responses to stimuli. His findings show some very interesting (and maybe initially counter intuitive) results. His study found that the babies that were more reactive to stimuli were much more likely to become introverts. The babies that were less reactive to stimuli were more likely to become extroverts. While watching the reaction of the children in the study, Kagan also recorded their blood pressure, heart rate, finger temperature and other indicators of the nervous system that are controlled by the amygdala, the "fear" control center of the brain. The extroverted babies, it seemed had a much less active amygdala, so a much lower fear reaction.

I think this goes a long way to suggest why extroverts might be less inclined to feel fear when speaking to people than introverts do. They simply don't have a strong reaction to fear in general. There are indications that this perception of risk also extends to other activities in life. Extroverts are also more likely to engage in high risk activities like sky diving, high impact sports, and are more likely to get speeding tickets.

Exploiting the amygdala can play a huge role in influencing (with a slant towards manipulating) people. In *Brain Bugs*, Dean Buonomano explores the rise of what he calls "amygdala politics", in which politicians exploit fears to win votes. As he points out, and as our simple survey demonstrates, fear has a powerful ability to override reason. The parts of our brains that deal with rationality, the parts that make us human, can be easily overpowered by the much older parts like the amygdala that we've inherited from our primitive animal ancestry. The neuroscientist, Joe LeDoux, put it this way "As things now stand, the amygdala has a greater influence on the cortex than the cortex has on the amygdala, allowing emotional arousal to dominate and control thinking".

Exploiting fear in a message to influence an audience is trivial. This is why the use of fear to influence in communication is so wide spread. Politicians, religious leaders, sales people and marketers all frequently attempt to pick at our insecurities and fears to motivate us towards certain actions. In World War II, Nazi propaganda relied heavily on xenophobia, fear of ethnic groups, to create an internal enemy that allowed the Nazis to solidify their control over the German people. Today, in the USA and other developed countries, fear of terrorism is a potent motivator to convince people that restructuring rights and privacy is necessary for security. Steven D. Levett and Stephen J. Dubner look at the numbers behind this fear in their book *Super Freakonomics*. They point out some interesting probabilities, based on U.S. census data. The average American has a 1 in 4 chance of dying from heart disease. Cancer will likely kill 1 in 7. The chance of dying in motor vehicle accidents is 1 in 88, accidental electrocution 1 in 4000, playing soccer 1 in 25000. The chance of dying in a terrorist attack currently stands at 1 in 69000 for a US citizen. This is clearly not a substantial risk. It's not terrorists you need to be afraid of; *it's cheeseburgers*.

Fear is not always irrational. Sometimes a risk is genuine, and so fearing it is completely reasonable. Parents even sometimes use fear to persuade their children. Tailoring a message to overcome fear is much harder. There are techniques we can use in communication to overcome the effects of fear. For example, instead of using negative "fearful" words that trigger a reaction in the amygdala, using words that connect to the cortex, like "rational", "thoughtful", "analyze" can sometimes influence people to be more critical in their thinking. Also, shifting a conversation away from assertive statements (or simple, rhetorical questions) towards genuine questions can also trigger a shift towards more rational thought. This works because it forces the audience to participate more in the thought process of the conversation, rather than just reacting to the message. As we'll see later on, asking questions is a powerful technique to influence the audience towards a point while encouraging them to think rationally.

Conditioning

How the audience perceives an idea is a consequence of the associative nature of the brain. The movie 'A Beautiful Mind' explored the life of John Forbes Nash, a brilliant Nobel Prize winning mathematician afflicted with paranoid schizophrenia. Nash's affliction might be described as an ability to see patterns in random noise; patterns that were not true, and not actually there. We actually all have this deficiency (or ability) to some extent. It's most evident when you look at optical illusions.

We've mentioned that the human brain is phenomenal at pattern recognition. It is not, however, always great at deciding what is true. So in general, it relies on consistency. If a series of events usually happens in the same way, we expect that they will always happen in the same way. When our brains find a new pattern in repeated events or stimuli, it's known as **conditioning**.

The classic example of this is Pavlov's famous experiment with his dog. Pavlov trained his dog to expect a treat when he heard a bell ring. At the conclusion of the experiment Pavlov's dog would begin to salivate in anticipation when he heard the bell, even before he was shown the expected treat, and even if he was *not* given a treat. The dog made the connection that the bell meant a tasty treaty, and made the perfectly reasonable assumption that if things happened a certain way before, they would continue to happen that way.

The associative nature is sometimes a detriment though, leading to illogical conclusions based on irrelevant information. *Brain Bugs* offers up another insightful example; an experiment conducted by physiologist John Bargh and his colleagues. They had volunteers come into the psychology building at the university where they worked for an interview. Before the interview, the volunteers were met in the lobby by one of the researchers and asked to carry cups of cold or hot beverages up to a second floor. There, the volunteers were interviewed by a second set of researchers using a series of misleading unrelated questions. As they left, the person in the lobby casually asked the volunteers to rate the friendliness of the interviewers on the second floor. The result showed that significantly more people that were given the hot beverage rated the interviewers as friendly, while the ones given the cold beverage were more likely to rate them as unfriendly. *The conclusion?* If you want people to like you, you should ask them to hold a warm drink on a cold day.

This idea stems directly from the associative nature of the brain. A pioneering neurosurgeon, Donald Hebb, first observed this in 1949, and coined the phrase, "Neurons that fire together, wire together" in his book *The Organization of Behaviour*. In essence, Hebbian theory suggests that if two stimuli are presented at the same time to the brain, they will become associated with each other. This nicely explains the root causes of Pavlov's dog's behavior. The dog's brain was conditioned to associate the ringing of the bell with food. It expected to get some tasty treat when it heard the bell.

Unfortunately, the associations that become wired in our brain are not always logically sound. Ringing a bell does not magically make food appear. Holding a hot or cold beverage does not change the demeanor or personality of people we meet. But our brain can fall into the trap of believing there is a connection between these stimuli, and that can be a problem. It's conditioning that makes us susceptible to the effects of framing. If we are unaware of these associations we've been conditioned to believe, then false cues can lead us to make incorrect decisions. They leave us vulnerable to manipulation by others.

I've seen this first hand. In my first year as a technical sales specialist, I had to lead a class to teach a group of perspective customers how to operate our product. The class was held at one of our partner's offices. We were expecting ten to fifteen people for this class, and I was concerned our room was going to be just slightly too small. We might be able to crowd in, but it would be a little uncomfortable. I asked the person coordinating the rooms if it was possible to switch to a slightly larger room.

Fortunately, I was travelling with Roger, our VP of sales, who surprised me by saying "No, this one's perfect." When the attendees arrived, as expected, it was just a little too small. People had to awkwardly shuffle around each other to reach their seats, and Roger had to stand awkwardly in the corner. But to my surprise, the session went very well, with ample discussion. Everyone provided positive feedback, and wanted to continue on looking at our product. Afterwards, Roger explained his reasoning; "A packed room means lots of interest".

I didn't appreciate it at the time, but this idea is firmly grounded in neuroscience. To the brain, if a topic is interesting, then a lot of people will be interested in it. If the room is crowded, then there are a lot of people. And therefore, according to our brains, if the room is crowded, a topic is interesting. And a high level of interest is automatically associated with a good presentation or product. This is not logically correct, but that's the brain we are saddled with. If we hear the right bell ringing, we will expect a treat.

There is a lot of irrelevant noise influencing how we perceive every message. You might have been told that you should "Never judge a book by its cover". This is perfectly logical. In an ideal world, we would judge people based on their actions and on what they say. But in reality, our brains are *wired* to judge books by their covers. We are wired to judge people on the way they look. This is not right, but it is an unfortunate fact of life.

This is another observation I can confirm from my own experience. During my time in technical sales, I noticed I actually had more trouble talking to customers when I visited them wearing a nice suit. Customers were more combative, and less inclined to trust me. Communicating complex technical points became much harder. On the other hand, if I wore slightly less formal attire, like jeans and a sport jacket, they seemed to trust me implicitly. I was a technical guy who knew what he was talking about rather than an intimidating businessman. Audiences were much more receptive and made an effort to listen to me when I wore jeans.

There's no better example of this than Apple's late CEO, Steve

Jobs. Jobs was famous for consistently wearing a black turtle neck and pants when he presented. I have heard that Jobs wanted the focus to be on the Apple products he was presenting, not his clothes. But this is, of course, not quite true. No doubt his audience did focus on the products he was presenting, but the black turtle neck and pants were very noticeable and distinctive. It helped establish a particular image of hipness and eccentricity, that audience's in-turn associated with Apple's products, making them the huge success they are today. By not wearing a suit and dressing down, Steve Jobs was trying to create a contrast from other CEOs, like Bill Gates. Intentional or not, his choice of apparel was very much a part of Apple's marketing. It helped influence the world in perceiving Apple products a certain way.

In communication, listeners should acknowledge the influence of irrational connections, and then work hard to focus on the message being communicated. This means being as logical and open minded as possible. Unfortunately, someone trying to communicate a message needs to be cautious of how he or she is being perceived. He or she may also need to make extra efforts to control the environment of the conversation and to present themselves as well as possible. Trivial influences, like the temperature of the room, appearance of a speaker or tone of words used to deliver a message can tremendously influence how a message is received.

Chapter Summary

- Our brains may make irrational connections. Things like a crowded room, a hot drink, or your physical appearance can influence how people perceive your message.
- Different word choices can also have a powerful effect on how people perceive your message, even when they do not change the objective meaning.
- Fear can be a powerful device to influence people. It often leads to irrational choices and beliefs.
- Fear can sometimes be counteracted by using words that encourage higher-level thinking.

Chapter 5: Consistency and Bias

When you think about it, the very fact that we can communicate ideas is pretty amazing. We start out with a set of thoughts in our brain. And when we want to, we can transmit these thoughts to some "device", hooked up to the brain, like our mouths or even our fingers. Then we can transmit ideas out into the external world in some physical form. From there, ideas can be picked up by some other device like an ear or an eye, and be "loaded" into someone else's brain. And if we do it right, that person ends up thinking the same thoughts we are!

The human brain is probably the most sophisticated and complex device known to science. Most people compare the brain to a computer (VonNeuman). This is tempting, because the brain stores memories, and a computer has memory. They certainly sound like they do similar things, but they could not be more different. The working of a digital computer's memory is, in essence, extremely simple and straightforward. A computer memory is an on/off switch. It's on, storing a 1, or it's off, storing a 0. Take that setup, and replicate it a billion or more times, and you have the memory of a modern computer. It's pretty simple. Each bit is grouped into sets of bytes (E.g. 8 bits together) and is given a particular address in the memory so it can be retrieved when necessary. This is all very discrete. There is no connection between one address and the next. If you want to know the state of a particular bit in memory, you don't need to worry about what other bits might be stored around it.

We don't yet fully understand the working of the brain (although we are making constant progress), but we know enough to conclusively say, this is NOT how the brain works. Unlike a bank of discrete switches, the brain stores information in the connections between neurons. At first glance, it's tempting to equate a neuron with a switch, because it sounds like one. It can fire, or it cannot fire. But the information is actually stored in the wiring of neurons together. Each neuron has tens of thousands of wires called *dendrites* (from the Greek word for tree) They reach throughout the brain and out into nerves, long distance telephone wires running throughout the body. It's these interconnections that make the brain work.

Before you were born, your brain started wiring these neurons together. As you grew, more and more connections were made, wiring associations between stimuli. Some connections wired in good associations, like the sound of your parents' voices and faces, with the feeling of comfort when receiving food or being held. Some connections wired in bad associations, like touching a hot stove and feeling pain. By the time people reach adulthood, they have 50 to 100 million neurons[6] in their brain, with over 1000 trillion connections, associating and encoding abstract concepts, emotions, fears, memories and basic sensations.

The brain is an astounding device for understanding the world. It allows us to make sense of a jumble of images, sounds, feelings, smells and tastes in way that even the most advanced computers cannot begin to approach. Recognizing how the brain functions can provide some helpful hints on how to communicate effectively.

Repetition

If you listen to people who are effective communicators, you'll notice they often repeat the main points of their message. There's a neurological basis for this. As someone is listening to a message, she is forming connections between neurons in her brain. If she hears a message more than once, those pathways actually grow and become stronger. The signals sent down them will fire more readily the next time she hears the same message. As this happens, the message becomes more familiar and easily recalled.

Neurologists have studied this phenomenon and discovered some important insights on how to improve how we learn. For example, some neurologists have suggested that if you are studying for an exam, and really want to remember a subject, it's best to study it at

---

[6] Estimates of the number of neurons in the brain vary wildly, from 10 billion to 200 billion. The bottom line is; **there's a lot of them.**

least twice or more, over a period of two days. This is far more effective than trying to cram everything into one intense study session the night before a test.

By repeating the material you have covered the day before, you reinforce the neural connections that make up the subject in your brain. This is known as the theory of 'Distributed Practice'. There are some strong indications that the process of sleep also plays a part in memory. Why we sleep is not completely understood, but it appears when the brain is asleep, it's actually doing "house cleaning". Sleep may be a mechanism by which the brain generalizes memories and ideas, and connects them. Taking a break for a nap in the middle of learning a new concept might actually be a good idea.[7]

Marketers have realized repetition is essential to make people remember their products. Commercials are often so repetitive for this reason. Coca-cola and Pepsi fight to be memorable, so that you automatically think of their brands when you go to buy carbonated sugar water. Product jingles are used to the same end. A catchy jingle can stick in your head all day. If you listen to the melody of the jingle in your head, you'll also listen to the words of the jingle in your head. This is how you'll end up strengthening the neural connections associated with the brand or product the jingle is promoting.

In World War II, Hitler used this trick to a terribly destructive end. Hitler understood immediately the powerful effect repetition in propaganda can have. Consider this chilling quote:

> *"The receptivity of the great masses is very limited, their intelligence is small, but the power of their forgetting is enormous. In consequence of these facts, all effective propaganda must be limited to a very few points and must harp on these in slogans until the last member of the public understands what you want him to understand by your slogan." - Adolf Hitler*

There is no doubt that repetition can have a powerful effect. Fortunately, it can be used for good purposes, to help people recall a valid fact, as well as evil ones like programming people to hate.

[7] Denise M Wechan, Rebecca L. Gomez, Department of Psychology, The University of Arizona, Dec 19, 2012.

I like to use repetition whenever possible, because it facilitates memorization. During presentations, I try to repeat core messages as much as possible without being redundant to help the audience retain them. Also, when presenting a training class over a few days, I try to repeat highlights of the important topics from the previous day. This not only helps remind people where we were in the class, but helps reinforce those concepts in the brain through repetition.

Nevertheless you should not overuse repetition. Once an audience has a message strongly wired in their brains, you won't hold their attention for long. People tend to tune out a repetitive commercial once they've heard it a few dozen times. They need some new content or contrast to hold their attention. Without it, they tend to stop thinking about a repetitive message. As we'll see next, the human brain equates consistency with truth. People can start to believe a message just because they have heard it so many times, and it happens to fit with what they already believe.

Consistency

The associative nature of the brain is significant when trying to communicate with an audience. The brain is never a blank slate. There are always existing ideas and concepts wired into the brain of the audience. This is critical to understand because the brain makes associations assuming that the world is consistent. Like Palov's dog, we expect things to occur just like they did in the past.

Consequently, if you present a new idea that seems consistent with all the other ideas the audience believes, then it's likely to be readily accepted. The strong wiring of the older existing ideas helps wire in the new idea. If you present an idea that seems in conflict with what your audience already believes to be true, it's highly unlikely they will listen to what you are saying. These existing ideas are sometimes referred to as a 'Cognitive Bias', and can be both a benefit and a hindrance.

It can be very beneficial to making your point if you can "hook-in" to the ideas already wired in the brain of the audience. Here's an example: if there is a historical figure that your audience greatly respects, find a relevant quote from that person to open a discussion on a difficult topic. This approach makes use of conditioning and cognitive bias, because thinking of someone who is revered can put the speaker in a thoughtful frame of mind. Your message will therefore be subconsciously connected to that frame of mind.

An even simpler example is to draw a connection between something the audience likes and your message. Most parents try to convince their kids to try fish at some time. Many use the line "Try it; it tastes sort of like chicken." This is essentially an attempt to hook into the cognitive biases of a child; chicken tastes good, and fish tastes like chicken, so fish will taste good.

There is a danger in doing this too much if the audience does not see a connection between the biases and your message. They may feel you are simply trying to exploit them. Most children do not think fish tastes just like chicken, so telling them it does might just undermine your credibility. People don't mind being influenced, but no one likes to be manipulated. The difference is in the perception of how true your message is believed to be.

This hints at how people assess if something is true or not. If there is a consistency in what you are saying with what they believe to be true, then they are likely to accept your message as truth. If there are glaring inconsistencies with what you are saying and what they already believe to be true, they will usually reject what you are saying. They may feel you don't make sense, or they may feel you are not telling the truth.

There is a limit to the ideas we can hope to convince another person of that's not based on how knowledgeable, eloquent or convincing we are. It is based on what someone already believes and how consistent we are with it. If what we are saying does not "connect" with any of his existing ideas, then it simply won't take hold in his brain. A radical new idea— one that challenges many of the established ideas is much more likely to be rejected.

We should recognize we all have cognitive biases. They may be inevitable to allow us to navigate the world without constantly questioning everything. They make up our identities. Religion is one obvious example. People do not say "I believe in the Hindu gods and the teachings of the Hindu religion" (to pick one at random). They say "I am Hindu". It's so much shorter! But it's also much more powerful and transformative. Rather than religion being an external subject to the speaker, the speaker becomes part of the religion, and vice versa. It suggests a *possible* cognitive bias, since the belief and the speaker have become so entwined that speaker has incorporated that label into their identity. If they encounter ideas or beliefs contrary to their own, they are much less likely to be receptive to them.

Since we're talking about communication, it's important to consider that when someone says "I am a [*insert label here*]", it is also a significant reduction of information. This is an important point which we will be discussing later in Chapter 10. Staying with Hinduism as an example, there are actually a wide set of possible beliefs that someone who describes themselves as Hindu might have. Hinduism is often studied by academics as a system of religions, rather than a single religion. Even within a single "version" of Hinduism, not all Hindus will share the same beliefs. And many Hindus will have beliefs that are not part of Hinduism. So when someone says "I am a Hindu", the speaker is giving you a general sense of what they believe, not a precise list of beliefs. If you really want to find out what they believe regarding a specific topic, you need to have a much deeper and more detailed conversation with them. This same issue comes up frequently in dealing with technical issues.

Politics also provides many obvious examples of cognitive bias, especially today in the United States. When someone says "I am a Democrat" or "I'm a Republican" they are admitting a cognitive bias regarding which political party is preferable. This is a concern; the idea behind democracy is that people should first weigh different candidates, without preconceived ideas about which should be better, and then choose which person to elect. Unfortunately, people with cognitive biases skip the "weigh different candidates" part, and immediately vote a certain way. They are, in effect, democratic dead weight. It also has a negative effect on political discourse. Instead of listening to politician's debate about specific policies or ideas with the desire to evaluate them, the voting public tends to prefer to hear politicians say things that reinforce the views and positions the voters already have. This is why it's good advice to avoid talking about politics or religion with a stranger. I especially follow this advice when traveling across the USA these days, because politics have become so polarized. It's become very hard to have a candid conversation without offending someone.

When someone has a deep cognitive bias that comes in obvious conflict with reality, the result is called *Cognitive Dissonance*. When it happens, the results can be both difficult to watch and occasionally hilarious. The U.S. 2012 election provided a wonderful and very public example. Karl Rove, conservative pundit of Fox News, provided a barrel of comic fodder for late night comedians when he demonstrated a severe case of cognitive dissonance on public television. Halfway through the evening, the Fox news research team announced that they were 99.95% sure incumbent Barack Obama had won Ohio, a strategic state that predicted the outcome of the election. Karl Rove, a life-long Republican, was clearly biased. Besides being employed by Fox News, he was also the head of a Mitt Romney's Super PAC, and a Republican strategist. The neural pathways in his brain were wired so strongly in favor of believing in a different outcome, that they could not adapt fast enough to accept the reality presented to him. So instead, he lashed out at his own team of analysts and statisticians on live TV.

Comedian Jon Stuart aptly described the situation as a television moment that "will… live forever"[8]. I was watching this live as well, and I do have to agree with Stuart; it was a truly memorable, funny, and slightly embarrassing, piece of television. Entertainment value aside, level-headed and rational minds must ask: What's the value of such a biased individual on a news show in the first place? If those who are in the business of delivering news cannot accept an obvious reality when it confronts them, how can they be relied on to communicate any reality in the news?

---

[8] http://www.newstatesman.com/world-affairs/2012/11/video-jon-stewart-describes-fox-news-election-night-coverage-crisis-bullshit-m
http://theweek.com/article/index/235979/karl-roves-epic-election-night-battle-with-fox-news-forecasters

Dean Buononmano in *Brain Bugs* cites a more morbid example from the end of the 18th century. At that time, the mortality rates of new mothers delivering babies in hospitals in Vienna was horrifically high. Post-delivery infections were claiming the lives of 20% of new mother's delivering in hospitals. In comparison, home deliveries by mid-wives in Vienna at the same time had a maternal mortality rate of 2%. The culprits turned out to be the doctors themselves. This was before the discovery of bacteria, so doctors did not understand the need to protect against germs by disinfecting themselves between operations. The doctors might go from dissecting dead bodies in the morgue to delivering babies, without washing their hands. Even after the discovery of bacteria and the possible connection to disease, some doctors simply refused to accept reality for several years. When the truth finally became undeniable, one doctor racked with guilt, committed suicide.

It had been impossible for the doctors to accept that they were responsible for the death of so many new mothers, or that they could be so wrong about how disease was spread. The transmission of disease by tiny bacteria was a new idea contrary to common sense at the time. *How could something so small like bacteria kill something big like a person?* Additionally, the guilt implied in accepting this new idea formed a strong cognitive bias some of the doctors could not see beyond.

I should point out; cognitive biases are not necessarily bad things. Adopting a simple label can help to summarize the vast and complex set of beliefs encoded in trillions and trillions of neurons. This is a simplification that is sometimes necessary for communicating an idea to another person, or even to ourselves. The problem with cognitive biases is that they can also impair our ability to listen, especially if we (or the person speaking to us) are *unaware* of them. To be an effective communicator, you absolutely must understand what cognitive biases you and your audience might have, and have a plan to manage them. Trying to directly challenge one of these biases in your audience will usually cause them to automatically dismiss you without listening to anything you are saying. And always keep in mind that this is also true when you are the audience. Becoming aware of someone else's cognitive biases requires some insight into their perspective, another feat made possible by our remarkable brains.

In my work as an IT professional, I often spend a lot of my time listening to people complain about software. Some of these people know what they are talking about, and have valid and very valuable points. But some do not. Some have issues because of a failure in understanding, because they are impatient, or maybe because they didn't sleep well the previous night. Sorting out the good points from the bad points requires careful listening to all of them.

The magical numerical wand

Some cognitive biases are so embedded in our brains and so universal, they can be extremely difficult to see. The effect of numbers on how people perceive a message is one example. Numbers can have an almost magical effect on a message. If I were to say, "Many methodologies agree the current stock market is overvalued" you might believe me, or you might not. I'm clearly stating my opinion on the subject. On the other hand, if I say "4 out of 5 methodologies agree the current stock market is overvalued", then suddenly my statement has much greater impact. Suddenly, I'm not just stating my opinion, I'm stating a *fact*. The natural assumption is that the statement reflects a well-documented study using sound techniques to reach a conclusion that is stated as a fact. We still might suspect that the fact is right or wrong, but we evaluate it as a much stronger and significant statement, because it triggers a much deeper response in our brain.

It's not hard to guess why this might be. The first things we teach our children are the alphabet and how to count. In fact, the ability to count is likely hardcoded to some extent in our developing fetal brains, and is likely very old. Some animals, such as common crows and dolphins, even share our ability to count to some limited degree. So the wiring to deal with numbers is very old and very well established.

Adding a number to a statement provides a hook into this ancient and rigid part of our brain. This is the source of its transformative power, and why it turns a statement from an opinion into a fact. Our brains automatically assume statements containing numbers are facts because of their association with numbers. This is why audiences are always hungry for numbers.

Later on, we'll examine the topic of truth in more detail, we'll see that most statements containing numbers are very precise, but usually end up being less accurate than more general statements without numbers. It can present a serious issue for geeks when they are trying to communicate something truthfully and correctly. In conversations about technical topics, statistics and numbers tend to always be fairly complex and qualified. Using them in conversation adds a huge burden of ensuring that they will be interpreted and understood in a way that is correct.

In my software development role, I often need to discuss performance characteristics. I often need to cover questions like "How much overhead will this solution add to our system?" Inevitably, there are two correct ways to discuss this topic. You could spend a long time going into details about a set of performance numbers, and explain in detail what each means. Or you could summarize the performance of a complicated system by saying "It depends" (on all the details involved). Both of these are usually unsatisfactory to an audience. They usually want to hear one simple magic number that they can easily remember, like 5% or 10%. The problem is this is usually not a "truthful" number because it is only a product of a certain specific set of conditions, and the question is usually general in nature. It's sometimes even a completely meaningless answer (5% of what?). What's fascinating in conversations is how an audience can forget almost everything that was said, except the statement with the number in it. Later, if the number was incorrect or doesn't seem to fit reality, this can come back to haunt the speaker. The audience often retains the number, but unfortunately forgets all the qualification and explanation that might have gone with it. The numbers are sticky, but the context they come with **is usually not**.

You can even exploit this stickiness of numbers to improve your own memory. The next time you are trying to remember names in a group of people, besides jotting down their name, try assigning a number to each name. Assigning a number allows you to plug into much older more established parts of your brain where concepts of numbers are encoded.

Dropping numbers in a conversation needs to be done with extreme caution, both because of the transformative way they turn opinion into fact, and because numbers can be extremely sticky. However, just like fear, using numbers is not always a bad thing. They can be a powerful way to help an audience retain and focus on a particular point. When truthful, they add great conviction to a message. The danger arises when they are, intentionally or otherwise, taken out of context. And in our communication, they are prone to be taken out of context.

Understanding Perspectives (and learning to lie)

We've already talked about the ability of our brains to transmit contained ideas, via symbols, to each other. This ability actually goes much, much deeper. We actually have a remarkable ability to imagine entire **perspectives** of other people. We can, in essence, build in our brains a model of what other people are seeing, hearing, feeling, in a given situation. It's almost as though we can construct a little copy of the other person's brain, in our own brain. Most interesting of all, research has shown that we don't actually have this ability at birth. It develops much later.

Life is pretty simple for the newborn human baby. Generally, a baby only requires the abilities to eat, sleep and poo. Most problems can be solved by crying about them until they are fixed. What a life! And neurologists have come to understand that, life really is pretty simple for the newborn brain. Babies, they have found, do not actually understand the possibility of other perspectives. They only understand and are aware of their own current perspective. To put it another way, they are completely self-centered. This manifests itself in a few ways. The first is the concept of **object permanence**.

Object permanence is the brain's understanding that just because you can't see something; it does not mean that it has ceased to exist. Babies do not understand that an object might be someplace else, because they do not understand concept of "someplace else". They only understand where they are, "here". Newborns do not like being separated from their parents because they don't understand that they might just be in another room. It's also why for a newborn less than 6 months, peek-a-boo isn't that much fun. Newborns just don't understand it.

Then at some point, after 6 months, the human brain begins to make some incredible leaps of abstraction. Suddenly, babies begin to find the game of peek-a-boo amusing. The disappearance and re-appearance of an object or face is suddenly quite novel and entertaining. This is the starting point of the baby realizing that even though they don't see something, it's still out there, somewhere.

Once babies begin to recognize object permanence, there is a second great leap in abstraction that comes typically 2 years later. This is when the toddler begins to realize that not only are there places they can't see "right now", there might be other perspectives they don't see "right now".

One experiment conducted with a group of three year olds demonstrates this ability. In the experiment, the three year olds were shown a block, and a transparent colored filter. The colored filter was then given to an adult, who would tell the child they were looking at the block. The three year old was then asked what color the block looks like to the adult. What is fascinating is that the three year olds consistently give the correct answer. They are able to construct a mental image of what the adult sees, and not confuse that perspective with their own. Two year olds in the same experiment consistently fail however. They always give an answer based on their current perspective. Two year olds, it turns out, really are self-centered, which is why parents struggle with "the terrible twos". Toddlers don't interpret their parent's point-of-view.

By the time we are adults, we are highly susceptible to the perspective of others. In fact, like framing, peer pressure exerts a powerful sway on our minds. We are all inherently programmed to try and fit in, even when we don't consciously realize it. In her book *Quiet*, Susan Cain recounts an experiment known as the "Asch" test, first conducted by Solomon Asch in the 1950s. The test involved a group of students who were told they were going to be given a vision test. The test consisted of three lines, one of which was clearly longer than the other. The test was simple enough that 95% of students gave correct answers on their own. Then the students were asked to answer the same questions as a group.

Unbeknownst to them, one student in the group was planted, and instructed to give incorrect answers. In a group, the rate of correct answers plunged to 25%, meaning 75% of the students went along with the student giving the wrong answer. This effect has been well studied. More recent studies in 2005 at Emory University conducted by neuroscientist Gregory Berns used a MRI scanner to track brain activity, and actually confirmed that the students in this experiment genuinely appear to believe the incorrect answer. So the opinions of our peers can have a profound effect on what we *think* we think.

While three year olds are generally more understanding of other people than two year olds, the realization that other people might have different perspectives also comes with an extremely clever and innovative ability. At three years of age, children generally develop the ability to tell lies. Now, lying is actually quite a remarkable feat. It requires conceptualizing not just what the truth is, but realising that other people might not know it, and that they could instead be persuaded to believe what you want them to, rather than just what is. This requires a lot of abstract thinking! What's more, to be believable, lies must be both internally consistent and consistent with what you imagine the person you are lying to believes. To do it well requires some hefty cognitive abilities.

So if you have a child, try to remember this the next time you catch him telling a fib. It is actually a remarkable demonstration of how cognitively gifted he really is. And fortunately, lying isn't the only skill that results from realizing other people can have different points of view. This is, in fact, a critical requirement for communicating effectively, which we'll explore in the next chapter. It's only by conceptualizing how our message will be received that we can tailor it to a particular audience. And in chapter 15, we'll explore the topic of truth and lying a little more deeply. We'll see that being completely honest is sometimes harder than you might think when you are trying to communicate.

Our brains, even with all their flaws and idiosyncrasies really are remarkable tools for understanding the world and communicating with one another. Like any complex tool, it helps to read the operating manual first, before you try using it. When we understand how the human brain works, we can tailor a message to facilitate retention. We can also be more believable and avoid negative associations. It can even allow us to compensate for our temperaments towards introversion or extroversion. And now that we have some insight into what is going on in our own heads, we can start to use the ability to imagine other people's perspectives we picked up as three year olds. We interpret what is going on in other people's heads when we are trying to talk to them.

Chapter Summary

- Introverts may actually think slower in conversations. They can compensate for this by anticipating and preparing for these situations. One way to do this is to think up responses to common questions ahead of time.
- Introverts may also struggle with short term memory, particularly remembering minor social details.
- Repetition is a powerful tool to aid retention. Repeating your main points will help your audience remember them. But be careful not to use this approach too much or your audience will become bored or stop thinking about what you are saying.
- Using numbers in a statement can have a strong transformative effect to increase the strength of the assertion. For this reason, numbers should be used with caution.
- Everyone has cognitive biases.
- People will accept ideas much more readily if they already fit with their cognitive biases.
- Cognitive biases can sometimes limit our ability to reason and adapt to reality.
- We all have an ability to imagine other people's perspectives. It's this ability that allows us to tailor a message to a particular audience, as well as to lie.

Chapter 6: The Audience

The former CEO of my start-up, Albert Lee, stresses the necessity of asking the right questions to your audience in his book *How to Meet the Queen*. Albert believes that this is one of the best ways to achieve your objectives in a conversation although to me it initially seemed backwards. After all how can you communicate what you want, by asking questions? Shouldn't you devote your energy to getting your message across rather than wasting time finding out things from the audience?

You might recall the story I told at the beginning of this book of the new VP that unintentionally offended and annoyed his audience. Understanding who your audience is obviously helps in avoid making serious social blunders that can get in the way of your conversation. But beyond this, understanding your audience is imperative to having them understand what you are saying.

To be honest, as a technical person (and a bit of an idealist) this is a concept that I was initially very resistant to. After a few years of reflection (and coaching from Albert), I think that the major stumbling block I had (and still sometimes have) stems from a belief in the objective nature of what I was trying to communicate. I like to believe that if something is true, it shouldn't matter who is saying it. Ideas should be independent, objective, and stand on their own. It's an absolutely logical assumption.

What I failed to grasp then was that having an idea and being able to communicate that idea are not the same thing at all. Ideas might exist in a physical form in people's brains in the wiring of neurons. But we don't have a way of directly dumping those structures from one brain to another. We need to deconstruct them into a set of symbols that are portable across the brain gap. To put it another way, when someone jots down a mish-mash of symbols, it's not the same thing as the idea itself. The effectiveness of the message containing an idea is highly dependent on the person it is being delivery to. Messages need to be tailored to people in the same way computer software is distributed in versions written specifically for a particular type of computer.

Know what your audience doesn't know

It's very hard, if not impossible, to communicate an idea in completeness. Your audience needs to have some experience or context to help them understand your idea. If you recall from the last chapter, the brain is highly associative. What seems like a concept that stands on its own is actually linked, in the brain, to a whole set of other concepts, facts and memories. And those concepts, facts and memories are linked to other concepts, facts and memories. This is what's known as an *infinite regress* in the math and software business. It can go on forever. So when we want to communicate an idea, how do we choose where the idea stops?

This is one reason why the idea and the message are separate yet inseparable. It's integral to think of the message in terms of what the audience can understand, rather than what you, the speaker, understands. Often when writing things down, I realize there are significant gaps in what I've said and what I was thinking. When you are "speaking to yourself" you don't notice these gaps, because the connections for them are already in your brain. What you were thinking, but don't say, remains in a blind spot.

In starting a conversation, a critical question to ask is "What is it that my audience does not know?" Asking this question helps expose these gaps in a message and shine a light into these cognitive blind spots. By figuring out what the audience already knows and doesn't know, you can figure out which neural "hooks" are present in the brains of the audience. We could potentially attach our message to these hooks, and use them to convey our message.

Geeks tend to fail in this regard a lot. Geeks usually understand technical things very well, but they tend not to understand what other people don't understand. One could make a comparison to the 2 year-old child that hasn't yet developed the ability to see things from other people's perspectives. I've fallen prone to this trap many times myself. Occasionally I'm stuck struggling in a conversation, because I've assumed the person I'm talking to must know something that they actually don't. This sometimes happened when I was talking to customers on certain IT subjects, and I realized the person I was talking to, who was typically knowledgeable and broadly experienced, lacked awareness of something I'd considered basic knowledge. This happens a lot in IT, where people tend to have very deep experiences with a particular set of IT vendors' products, but little experience outside that set. For example, people who are computer experts and use the Windows operating system a lot usually don't know much about the basic operation of Linux computers, and vice versa.

What is most surprising is that it's often the people who are closest to you that might lack the insights you have on a subject without you realizing it. It's natural to assume that when you judge something to be obvious, the people you are closest to will also see it. But this is often not the case.

When you are working as a team with someone, or a group of people, it's natural to divide up work so each team member carries some of the work. It's also natural to give each team member different work, and to assign work that suits each team member's abilities. The result is a divergence in experience. As an example, I work in an engineering department, and spend a lot of time talking to customers. I tend to develop a lot of insight into what problems customers face, because I hear customers tell me the same things over and over.

Conversely, the developers on my team don't talk to customers as much. They spend their days working very hard to solve the technical challenges necessary to address customer's problems. They tend to develop a really good sense of these technical challenges, and have a lot of insight into which problems are possible to solve, and which are not. It's very easy for either developers or myself to assume the other knows what the customer's problems are, or what the challenges are in addressing that problem and if it's possible to solve them. However this isn't the case. The only way to share this experience is to make a continuous effort to communicate to share these experiences.

Who your audience is matters

It drives me crazy when someone who is required to

communicate with other people, completely neglects the audience's identity. In my line of work, I am what is known as a "subject matter expert" on a particular set of software products. You might assume this means people would come to me with questions about them, which does happen on occasion. But mostly, they just want my PowerPoint slides. I do keep a large set of PowerPoint slides to cover almost any purpose and audience. So when I get asked for a set of slides, I immediately ask "Sure…who's your audience?".

Unfortunately, more often than not, the person requesting the slides will have no clue how to answer this question. They just want any old slides to show, without actually having put any thought into what they are trying to communicate, or *to whom* they are trying to communicate. The results are usually painful to watch. I've seen presentations that I create to train our internal level 3 support staff presented to customers as sales material. Sales presentations do not go well with slides that only discuss what might go wrong with your product. I've seen technical deep dives given to potential investors that have never touched an IT system themselves and could not spell SQL (a language used in databases). This leaves the audience bewildered. I regularly see marketing slideware presented to technical folks who are trying to figure how to make the software work in specific situations. These presentations are *always* train wrecks, because the audience wants to go deeper and becomes annoyed when they don't. The person presenting needs to think about who they are trying to present to. To communicate effectively, this must be the starting point to every conversation.

It's also important to recognize that what an audience knows can be as big a source of confusion as what they don't know. If you attempt to use a word or term that they are familiar with in a completely different context, they might subtly mistake your meaning. This sort of confusion can be very difficult to sort out, because it's not immediately apparent. Technical conversations are particular prone to this problem. Software products, like databases for example, all do similar things, and use similar names for things. But the details of how they do it are often quite different. When different things sound the same, you need to spend extra time calling out what is different. Having a conversation with someone who has lots of experience with one software product about a similar, but different software product can be extremely confusing for this reason.

Here's an analogy. If you travelled to a foreign country, where everyone only spoke a language you couldn't understand, you would expect to have trouble communicating. Even trivial conversations would become brain teasers. In my youth, I spent a few months traveling through India, from the north to the south. Some of the time, this journey took me through some parts where English speakers were rare, and I had to rely on hand gestures and head nods. Unfortunately, even nodding of the head for 'Yes' and 'No' is not a universal expression. Instead it might be a bobble (but whether that might be a 'Yes' and 'No', I'm still not sure). In other parts of India I travelled, English was common…but *different*. Words did not have the same connotation, or were used in odd ways.

Pick a common language

When it comes to communicating with others, we are all travelers in foreign countries, even though we don't always realize it. Sometimes the language we use often seems to be the same, but the ideas and assumptions behind them are different. Sometimes, especially when discussing technical topics, we actually are speaking a completely foreign language, using words which might seem strange and nonsensical to other people. In order for a speaker and an audience to understand each other, they need to overcome this language barrier, and find some common set of symbols to communicate their ideas.

At times, the analog of a foreign language is closer to a literal truth. In his book *How to Meet the Queen*, Albert Lee points out that every high-tech company has completely different words and terms for the same thing. Having now worked with Albert and dealt with a long list of high tech companies myself, I can attest that this is true and can be tremendously frustrating. Sometimes, it's tempting sometimes to drop the pretext of figuring out the local terminology and revert to basic (E.g. "Can you please take me to the person that fixes stuff when it's broken?"). But if you are ever in a position to do business with these companies, it's essential you use the right local dialect, otherwise you will immediately be perceived as an outsider. You also might miss subtle differences in how the people at the company understand things.

This is a true challenge. It seems like a chicken and egg problem - how can you understand your audience *before* you get to know your audience? The answer, as it is with learning all new languages, is with patience and some common frame of reference to start with. As Albert explains in *How to meet the Queen*, the best place to start is to ask a lot of questions to the audience you are trying to communicate with. By asking questions, you can begin to map out what terms the audience uses, what topics they are interested in, and what experience or prior knowledge they might have with your subject. All of these things help establish a common language you can use with your audience to effectively communicate your message.

In a technical discussion between technical people, speaking "the same language" is important. Different technical disciplines develop their own languages that are best suited to communicating within their own field. Speaking to another technical person outside that field requires making an effort to use common terms and ideas that both you and that person understand. My background is in software development, particularly in databases, so I understand IT subjects a certain way and most frequently use terms that are database-centric. Occasionally, I need to work with a system administrator. They tend to use a completely different set of terms and lingo to describe things.

The problem arises when they are talking to someone else and don't realize they are using terms that the audience will not understand, or will misinterpret. Again, in the high-tech world, both of these are extremely common. Acronyms, for example, proliferate in high-tech businesses. This is natural, since people don't want to always list out long names for things. But if you are talking to someone that doesn't know what the acronym stands for, they are completely cryptic and devoid of meaning. Similarly, some words are so common they've become devoid of meaning. I have a personal vendetta against the word *'management'*. Almost every piece of software today is described as something that does *'management'*. This could mean it monitors something, it schedules something, it stores something, or maybe it allows you to view something. The *'management'* term is so ubiquitous that it's nearly impossible to figure out what a software product does without more information.

So careful consideration must be given when using ambiguous words and terms to ensure they actually convey some useful information to an audience. And this attention needs to take into account *who* the audience is. When speaking to experienced colleagues in a business setting, you can usually be more relaxed about using special terms than when you are talking to someone else. When speaking to someone at another business, extra caution should be given before you use the same terms, to clarify what they mean. And when speaking to someone socially, you should probably assume they are not going to know what you are talking about. It's also important to recognize that if an audience is less familiar with certain technical terms, it might be intimidated by them. If it is intimidated by them, it may immediately recoil from the conversation. So where possible, it always helps to convey a message using terms that the audience is comfortable with.

This approach does come with its own dangers however. Using metaphors, for example, can be greatly misleading. When one infamous metaphor, "*The internet is a series of tubes*", went viral, it earned Texas senator Ted Stevens a heap of disrespect from geeks. The saying actually became a rallying cry for those opposed to Stevens' agenda, because the internet is, most definitely, *not a series of tubes*. I've encountered this problem myself, when sales people have favored the analogy "*It's like a traffic cop*" to describe a software product we were selling. While that painted a favorable picture most people readily seemed to understand, it was significantly misleading. Often, once they did appreciate what the software did, they would remark at how wrong that statement was. To be fair, it was "*like a traffic cop*", in some very limited ways, but like all metaphors, this one had limits. The software did not, for example, take coffee breaks or go home at the end of the day. So it wasn't exactly like an average traffic cop.

So when it's not possible to get by with a simple metaphor or term the audience is familiar with, it's sometimes in the speaker's best interest to make the audience feel as familiar and comfortable with new technical terms. Speakers can do this by explicitly defining these terms, and working with the audience to make sure they are correctly understood. This will go a long way to making the audience feel more comfortable. It's also helpful to use repetition, by periodically reminding the audience what the terms mean, so that its understanding does not drift over time.

Once an audience is familiar with a particular term, it's important to make sure you stay consistent and don't drift away from it. Don't use different terms for the same thing. This is an area where I think both geeks and non-geeks fail equally. I've observed that non-geeks tend to avoid using the correct technical terms because they don't feel confident they understand them or they don't see the difference between them and other terms that sound the same. Geeks, on the other hand, can sometimes switch terms because they feel they can invent a better term on the spot for what they are trying to say. Unfortunately, this is completely self-defeating; switching words around only leads to confusion about what they are talking about.

This is also a significant problem in large groups. For everyone to understand each other in the group, it's important to use consistent terms. Nevertheless, since each person is involved in the same activity it's often possible to rely on context to get by. The real problem arises when individuals in the group communicate with people outside the group. One group member might use one term to describe something, while a second member might use a completely different term. The result is that the external audience can get a jumble of many terms, without any context to sort them out, and end up completely confused. This happens all the time in large IT projects.

There's an even more basic failure on the part of both geeks and non-geeks. Discussing a complex topic can require a lot of energy. It's natural for people to get tired, and start to take short cuts in their message, which can make it very imprecise and confusing. Besides using acronyms without explaining what they mean, people may let pronouns (like "he", "she", "that", "the") creep into a conversation, pushing out proper nouns that are specific. It's easy when you are tired to start referring to everything as "That thing". Pronouns are short forms that make conversation more fluid, but they rely on the audience having a solid context in their minds for what you are talking about. If listeners lack that context, they can easily get lost because these words provide none. They do not help people understand what you are trying to say. Recently at work, a colleague asked me out of the blue "Is it okay to restart the database?" Looking at a diagram of the environment we were working in, I pointed out there were 6 different databases servers, and I had no clue which one he meant. He replied, "Oh, sorry, of course, you're right. I meant the one that needs to be restarted...should I restart it?"

Again, this comes up a lot in software design. Complicated software products always have log files containing information and error messages, written by the developers, that indicate what the software is doing and if there were any problems. When something goes wrong or breaks, there is usually a message written to some log file *somewhere*. So developers are fond of saying "Just check the logs" to users and support people, or anyone else trying to make sense of the problem when the software doesn't work.

It's usually not obvious which log to check to find the messages for an issue if there is more than one log file. And it's also usually not obvious which messages in the log might be relevant to a particular issue and which aren't. And, more often than not, these log messages are useless and incomprehensible to anyone besides the software developer that wrote them, because the developer didn't really write them for anyone else to understand. He only wrote the messages for himself.

It takes a few years of experience to comprehend why this is a really bad idea. First, if you are the only one that understands something, then you are inevitably going to be the one that gets a call in the middle of the night to help sort out some problem. Perhaps some people enjoy this. I do not. Second, I've occasionally been asked to help look at problems in software I wrote 10 to 15 years ago. It's amazing to look back at some of the messages and comments on these occasions and wonder "*What did I mean by that*!?". The problem in these situations, of course, is that messages I had written were written for my much younger self, and I now lack the context to fully understand them. When I had written them, I should have included a little more

83

background with the message to fill in that context.

Finally, it's important to recognize that the choice of words used in a conversation can also be used to strongly influence (or manipulate) the audience. We've seen in the previous chapters how negative or positive words can be used to frame a message. And I mentioned the example of my well-spoken boss, who used a quote from Star Wars to convince me that an unwanted business trip was a necessity. This is an example of choosing the right language for the target audience (in this case, me) to make sure the message was received.

Audience Manipulation

This tailoring of language and words to an audience can be extremely powerful. In technology businesses, words are often targeted to suggest a particular solution. If you describe every problem as a nail, it's easy to convince someone they need a hammer. Consequently, a hammer salesperson will often describe every problem as a nail.

At the time I'm writing this book, where I live in Toronto, our mayor Rob Ford has regularly been making the international news, for all the wrong reasons. He was videotaped smoking crack cocaine, uttering death threats in a drunken stupor, has numerous proven connections to a notorious Toronto gang, has previously been charged with drunk driving, has been accused of assault, has been accused of *sexual* assault, is possibly implicated in blackmail and death threats, and has generally acted in a fashion that is *spectacularly* unbecoming of a civic leader (the list actually goes on much longer, but you probably get the point). His relationship with local news outlets has gone from antagonistic to what could be described as complete and open warfare, and has launched a series of lawsuits (with almost no chance of success) to retaliate against the media reporting on his alcohol and drug related antics.

So if you don't live in Toronto, you might be wondering, how someone so obviously off-the-rails can manage to still have a notable approval rating. And even potentially have a shot at re-election? (Even if you do live in Toronto, you might be wondering the same thing). One of the answers is his disciplined and calculated use of one single word. In all his public addresses, from his campaign speeches, to his teary apologies for his lewd and disgraceful behavior, Rob Ford addresses the people of his city as "*taxpayers*".

If you think about it, this is an odd choice of words. The people who live in a city are *citizens*. So why consistently use the word "Taxpayers"? The answer is, of course, Mayor Ford's one-dimensional election platform revolved solely around cutting taxes (well, ok, and getting tough on drugs and gangs). He uses the word taxpayer because he wants people to think of themselves as taxpayers, and only as taxpayers, not as citizens. The words are a calculated choice to influence the perspective of his audience into evaluating everything by that one simple metric, "how much am I going to pay in taxes?" If that's the only thing his constituency uses to evaluate his performance, a mayor who is a drunken crack addict might arguably have a shot at re-election. This particular word choice has an impressive ability to bend reality to make Rob Ford seem like a sane choice, in spite of Torontonians already having a lower tax rate than almost every other major city in North America (a fact that Rob Ford actually bragged about on The Tonight Show). Ford's singular impressive use of word choice is not just a great example of influencing an audience based on who they are; it's an example of a speaker convincing the audience *of who it is*.

Chapter Summary

- Understanding your audience is critical to communicating effectively. You cannot communicate a message in the same way to all audiences. You need to make the message fit the audience.
- Do your research on what will offend your audience. Do not assume you can talk freely about any subject, particularly politics, religion, war and even sports.
- Don't make assumptions. Ask yourself: What does the audience not know? What does the audience know? Then, don't focus on communicating what you know. Instead communicate *what*

the audience does not know.
- Consider that the people you work with might not have the same experience or exposure that you do.
- You need to find a common language to successfully communicate with your audience. Beware of words and terms that won't mean anything to your audience. Beware of ambiguous terms that will be misunderstood. Teach the audience new terms when necessary. Repeat them a few times to aid retention.
- Beware of metaphors that are unclear and misleading.
- Be consistent in the terms you use. When you are working in a large group, make sure everyone agrees on a set of terms to use when communicating with people outside the group.
- Be cautious of what your audience already knows, because it can lead to confusion if they can't reconcile it with what you are saying.
- Beware of pronouns (like "he", "she", "that", "the"). Be explicit to avoid confusion.
- Understand that every time you write something, you are writing for someone else (even if the someone else is you).
- Be conscious of when someone is trying to manipulate you by telling you what you want to hear.

Chapter 7: Channel Capacity

Channel capacity is a borrowed term in cognitive psychology. It originally came from electrical engineering. There, it's a measure of how much information can be transmitted over a particular medium (a wire, radio wave, or sound wave) in a certain amount of time. [9]

Channel capacity in cognitive psychology means something very similar. It describes how much a person can understand in a particular message. The key element implied in this definition is still time. Upon hearing an explanation of some subject, some people will immediately comprehend it. Some people will take much longer. If the concepts are novel to them, they will need more time to think about it. More time to build connections in their brains. This doesn't mean they won't get it however. It only means the rate at which the information is delivered needs to be tailored to how fast they can receive it.

If you spend a lot of time with people from different parts of the world, you'll notice that people from some cultures tend to speak very quickly, and others tend to speak very slowly. This can make it challenging for someone from a fast speaking culture and a slow speaking culture to communicate, even when they are speaking the same language. However if the faster speaker slows down, then suddenly they have no problems communicating.

Channel capacity imposes three limits on conversations that can impact how successful you are at communicating. First, it limits the speed of communication. Your audience can only absorb concepts at a certain rate. If you go too fast, you will leave your listeners in the dust. Second, your audience has limited time and patience to listen to you. ~~That means you can only go so~~ far in a single conversation, and the

[9] Bandwidth is closely related to channel capacity. The common usage of the term bandwidth is better described as channel capacity. The fact that a term like bandwidth *is* a popular term, one that is part of the vernacular for both young children and senior citizens, is a reminder of how important technology is today.

time you have to get to a point is limited. The third limit we will return to in the next chapter.

So what happens when you exceed someone's channel capacity? In short, your message won't get through. Trying to explain too much too fast will leave an audience with its heads spinning. This is especially problematic for the conversation because it's natural for people to become frustrated and stop listening altogether if they don't immediately understand what you are saying,. To admit that you don't understand something or that someone is going too fast for you to follow requires both patience and humility. Similarly, if you talk for too long, people will stop listening to you. They may even forget what you had previously said.

If your job is to explain a complicated technical concept, channel capacity is a very pertinent issue. It can be especially difficult because, by definition, someone who is a technical expert has the framework to understand a specific topic that is uncommon. If they are speaking to an audience, she can't rely on her own framework to communicate ideas. She needs to base her message on some framework for understanding things, such as an analog or metaphor that the audience already has, or she needs to spend valuable time constructing a framework to understand the topic by filling in the background the audience is lacking. Both approaches have risks, which we'll discuss later.

Figuring out the existing framework of an audience, or in other words, what people already know, can be a real challenge. With coworkers, family and friends, you usually have a sense of their past experiences. You can guess what topics they understand or don't understand. But when you walk into a room full of strangers, it takes some exploration to map out exactly what they already know. Not all audiences are helpful in this regard either. There is always an element of egotism to be wary of. During my years doing technical sales, I'd often hear managers of potential customers tell me "My people are experts; you can skip all the background and just get to the details". This was usually a sure sign that I would need to spend more time on developing a background, because once we started it would usually become apparent the audience didn't have a clue about the topic we'd be discussing. The audience can often greatly over estimate its own channel capacity, which can be limited by their patience and lack of background knowledge. It's natural that an audience would not necessarily know what background information it needs to have before discussing a topic. After all, if the audience already knew what the message was, it wouldn't need to hear it.

There is a trade-off to spending too much time establishing a common framework by discussing background information to a topic however. Everyone has a limited amount of patience to listen to a message, a maximum time they are willing to share with you. This limits the total amount of channel capacity for each person in the audience. If a speaker takes too long to get to his point, he will lose the audience before he gets a chance to say it.

Not dumbing it down

It's easy to see there would be consequences for going too fast or taking too long when communicating a message to an audience. So if you have a complicated message, as is often the case, how do you work around this? There is an instinct in many geeks that the only way to do this is to "dumb down" the message. This implies leaving out information or simply lowering it to a level that the audience can understand.

As Mark Henderson writes in his book, the *Geek Manifesto*, many geeks find this distasteful, and this is why they tend not to engage in topics like science and technology outside their own circles. I think the issue here however, is with the geeks. Understanding this process as "dumbing down" represents an attitude that is both immature and unproductive. It is one of the major stumbling blocks that limits the influence of geeks. I contend that the basic mechanics of this approach are correct, but the understanding and attitude of it are completely wrong for a number of reasons.

The first problem is that it originates from an illogical position. If the speaker has a message to share on a topic, it's only reasonable to assume that the listeners don't already know that message or the background to the message. If they did, then the speaker would have nothing of value to say. It represents arrogance in speakers, implying that they are an expert in all topics. They are "smart" and their audience is "dumb". This is unrealistic, of course. No one can be an expert in all topics. There will be topics the audience is more versed in. In fact, given the bi-lateral nature of communication we've been talking about and the importance of knowing the audience, a smart speaker should spend as much time figuring out what the audience *doesn't* know as the audience spends figuring out what he knows. Finally, this attitude is poisonous. It is usually obvious when a speaker holds the audience in contempt. The result is the audience becomes hostile to the speaker, and the speaker fails to convey his topic. Not so smart after all...

Here's an example. Einstein's theory of relativity provides a more accurate model of the movement of bodies with mass in a gravitational field than Newton's "Law" of gravity. And we now have observational evidence that even the more strange predictions of relativity are correct (from experiments on the Gravity Probe 'B' satellite). So why do we still teach Newton's Law of gravity when we know it's "Wrong"? Why aren't all school children just taught relativity right from the start?

There are two reasons. The first is that Newton's law is not "Wrong". It is less accurate. It works in most situations, but not in all. The concept of precision and accuracy is an important one we'll discuss in Chapter 14. Newton's law is also a lot easier to understand. The math is much simpler, and the concepts are straightforward. Most people can understand it. Things that have mass attract each other. It does not require you to wrap your head around crazy concepts like accelerating frame of references. Relativity is much more complicated and much harder to understand, so far fewer people can understand it. By teaching Newton's law to everyone, we are making a choice about how much they need to know. Reducing the information delivered so it fits within their channel capacity, while still providing a good description of the world. Of course, if they need a deeper understanding (Relativity), after first understanding the initial message (Newton's Law), then that can be a second conversation.

Being too precise

There is an art, however, to making the right choices about what information is critical and needs to be included in a message, and what information should be left out for the sake of clarity. This is a task that many technical people struggle with. Geeks are usually good with breaking the big picture down into details in order to understand them. They often can be very *precise* in what they say. In science, *precision* describes how detailed a measurement is (E.g., 1/16 of an inch). Accuracy, on the other hand, describes how often a measurement is correct (E.g., 9 times out of 10). Precision and accuracy often get confused because they are always linked together. As you get more precise, it usually becomes hard to stay accurate. And usually, a reading that is very precise is useless unless it is also accurate (correct most of the time).

Geeks tend to be very precise, detail oriented people. Unfortunately, this can create problems for them when they try to communicate. They will often attempt to communicate ideas as precisely as possible, which can make their message harder for an audience to understand. You could describe this difficulty as a loss of accuracy because of the cost of precision in the message. Many geeks don't immediately see this as their problem because they tend to believe that what they *said* was accurate. Unfortunately, they usually don't consider if what was *heard* was accurate.

Consider this conversation, I once overheard between a sales person and a software developer:

Salesperson: "Is it possible to add support for this?"

*Software developer: "***Yes***, it's technically possible. But it will be extremely difficult, and will not work in some important cases. It will probably not be very reliable either. Also we don't actually have enough developers to take this on, and we're already overcommitted."*

Salesperson : "Ok, Great, I'll tell them we think it's possible."

*Software developer: "***Wait, no***, that's not what I said...that's not a good idea..."*

I've sadly heard this conversation many times over the years. Some non-geeks are very fixated on the big picture; so fixated that when someone provides them with unwanted details, especially technical details, they immediately filter them out. I'm sure if I could look inside the mind of the sales person in this conversation they would have heard it like this:

Salesperson: "Is it possible to add support for this?"

Software developer: "It's technically possible. Blah blah blah, blah, blah blah…"

Salesperson : "Ok, Great, I'll tell them we think it's possible."

Software Developer: "blah blah blah…Good idea!"

The objectives of each conversation obviously play a powerful role. The salesperson in this conversation had a strong vested interest in having the software developer say yes. His objective was probably very clear in his mind, since he had a lot to gain financially from that outcome. The software developer, on the other hand, should have been motivated by the fear of overcommitting. Instead he was trying to be as informative as possible. That was not the right objective in the given situation. Correctly managing expectations should have been the main goal.

A better way to handle this would have been for the software developer to clearly say "No". This is a much less precise answer, and lacking in information. It is nonetheless more accurate, because it clearly expresses the essence of what the software developer was trying to say. Why couldn't the developer do it? It's unfortunate, but geeks in particular have a tremendously hard time saying "No, it will not work". They always want to say "It will work, **but** blah blah blah…*so, it will not work*". It possibly stems from a need to always seem capable. Or perhaps it's a struggle to let go of an imaginary ideal and face reality. But if something will likely not work well the answer to the question "Will it work?" should be "No. It will not". It's an accurate, honest and clear answer.

By not leading with a "No" response, the software developer was leaving his implied conclusion to the end of their message. This ignores what we call the 'Writers pyramid', which we'll discuss in the next chapter. It also ignored the channel capacity of the sales person, who had no interest or context to understand the technical details. This is perfectly normal. When people get stressed, are short on time, have other concerns, or even just need to go to the bathroom, their attention span goes way down. It's not usual for a manager to have a shorter attention span for the people who work for him or her. So you should carefully consider; if your boss asked you a question, do you want the first word to be reflective of how you really feel about something, or the opposite?

The software developer also ignored the potential effect of his audience's objectives, which was to get a "Yes". Objectives can powerfully influence how a message is interpreted. The audience sometimes knows what it wants to hear. In a high-tech company, when a sales person asks an engineer if their product can support something, he usually wants to hear "Yes". Sales people are typically incented to sell with financial rewards. There might be tens of thousands of dollars to encourage them to hear "Yes" to a question if it means they can pursue a sale. In these cases, if the engineer gives them an ambiguous or oblique answer, the sales person will naturally favor a positive answer. It's the nature of their profession to be optimistic, and assume that problems will be overcome.

The instinct to be very precise can cause an issue another way. When geeks get hung up on the details of a topic, they can lose perspective on the "big picture". Here's another conversation I heard while working at our start-up. This was an exchange between one of our technical pre-sales people and a software developer:

> *Pre-sales person: "Most of our customers are only interested in JDBC applications. We need to focus on improving our support for them."*
>
> *Software developer: "No, that's wrong. customer A is using ODBC. We need to spend time on that."*

So who was right in this exchange? That's a bad question. Both people were "right" in some sense. You could say the software developer is very right, because he made a precise statement about a single customer. The pre-sales person however, was making a less-precise general statement about *most* customers. His statement was very accurate, but less precise. The software developer missed this point, because he could not switch his frame of reference away from thinking about a single customer to most customers. He could not distinguish between an exception and the general rule.

Why geeks tend to focus on details is understandable. It's usually the details of a topic that hold the interesting bits. The special cases and exceptions are what make problems challenging. So it's the details that geeks devote most of their internal energy on. But just because these details are the most challenging to deal with does not mean they are automatically important. Their importance can only be assessed by understanding their impact on the topic as a whole. Therefore, understanding the whole is critical to keeping details in their proper perspective.

...but the devil's also in the big picture

The first step to keep the proper perspective on details in a conversation is to recognize that some points are key elements whereas others are details. When you have a large set of points to make, it sometimes helps to assign a value to how "general" each point is. The most general points are usually the ones that need to be communicated first and with greatest emphasis. Once they have been communicated, then you can start to add in details. If you are discussing something that is an exception to a rule, make sure your audience understands the rule first, and then explain the exception. Lead with the general case, then the specific. Remember that if your audience tunes out at some point, it's probably more important that they hear and retain the big picture, rather than only recalling discussions about a particular detail.

And when you are down into the details, keep reminding the audience of where they fit. Give them the perspective to understand the detail. If something is true 1 time out of 10, phrase every sentence to reinforce that ratio, so it doesn't get lost in the minds of the audience. It's important to understand that the natural instinct of the audience will be not to gauge the importance of a detail by what is said about it, but *how much* is said about it. If you spend much more time discussing a fine point of a topic, it's highly likely it will be remembered as an important point.

Developing the proper perspective on details is not just up to the speaker. As a listener in a conversation, it's possible to keep a firm grip on where details fit by asking the speaker to frame them in some context. For example, one could ask "How often does that occur?" or "How common is this?" Asking questions like this keep details from becoming the big picture in a conversation.

Talking to multiple audiences at the same time

If you are trying to reach a single person, understanding your audience and targeting a message to her is usually straight forward. You can chat with her for a few minutes, and develop a pretty good understanding of her background, what she knows, and what she doesn't. Even when you are trying to reach a larger group of people with the same background, this is usually not too difficult, if you can assume they all have similar experiences. But when there are many different types of people in the room, understanding the audience and targeting a message at them can be more challenging.

If each person in the audience has a different background, finding a common framework that reaches all of them can be difficult. The wider the audience, the more common the language the speaker needs to use to reach them. Each person will also have a different channel capacity, so the pace at which they can follow a complicated message will vary, as well as their patience.

Sometimes, when faced with an audience of different types of people in a business setting, I like to explicitly break the audience into groups, and address them separately. This is a technique that usually works well, because it explicitly acknowledges the differences in the audience, while making it clear that everyone in the audience is valuable.

Occasionally when you are doing a business presentation, there is one special person in the audience that you know you want to influence. In a sales presentation, this might be the CEO or CIO. In most business situations, it's usually these key people that actually make decisions. In order to influence a decision at the organization, it's critical to engage these people with the message so they understand the value of what is being said. It's also important to recognize that these people are also typically very busy people who have short attention spans. Any attempt to communicate a message to them typically needs to be brief and concise. In these situations, I always try to address the people in this part of the audience. I expect a CEO in the room will listen for the first 30 seconds...and then tune me out. I wouldn't expect the CEO to follow the whole discussion.

It's tempting to tailor the message in this situation to only target that one special person, and ignore the rest of the audience. I think this is a real gamble though. Usually, when someone else in the audience feels left behind in a discussion they will try to raise questions in an attempt to get something of value out of the discussion. This can derail the speaker's message because it disrupts the order of the message. It can also reduce the channel capacity of the audience as a whole by taking up valuable time. It also important to understand, even if a CEO is no longer paying attention to what the speaker is saying during a presentation, he or she will still be paying attention to the mood of the other people in the room. If the rest of the audience is happy and engaged in the discussion, the CEO will have a good impression of the speaker and their topic. If someone in the room is clearly not happy, the CEO will pick up on that, and associate that with the presentation. As we've seen in Chapter 3, even if the speaker's message is compelling, their message can be harmed by an irrational negative association. Always try to create and maintain a positive atmosphere.

Handling questions in a positive way is extremely important. It's good to remember that questions are almost always a good thing. They usually mean the audience is genuinely interested, even if the questions seem hostile, or nonsensical. If you do get side tracked in a presentation by questions that are either too in depth to discuss, or just plain don't make sense, a good way to handle them is to request that you talk directly with the person who asked them after the presentation. Social pressure will ensure that most people will accept this without complaint. And in a narrower discussion, you can hone in much better on what the person really wants to know.

Chapter Summary

- The channel capacity of an audience limits how much information you can give them. Audiences can only understand a fixed amount of information in a period of time. They have limited time and patience to listen to you.
- If you exceed the channel capacity of an audience, they will leave the conversation confused or forget what you said.
- Try to figure out the channel capacity of the audience on your own. If someone is an expert on a topic, it's usually obvious. Even if someone claims he or she is an expert, he or she usually is not. Use dialogue and your own judgment to discern if someone is actually an expert on a topic.
- Never "Dumb down" a message. Instead try to provide the right level of detail, using the right terms for your audience. Never assume that an audience is stupid because it doesn't know what you are trying to communicate to it. Instead, vary the precision of your message to suit the audience.
- Lead with your most important points, so your audience will still hear them even if they stop listening.
- Always provide context to your audience first, and then fill in details second.
- Keep details in perspective by reminding the audience of their context.
- Mixed audiences can present special challenges. Recognise that the people in a mixed audience will potentially have different channel capacities - different attention spans, and different background knowledge. An effective communicator will try to reach everyone in the same conversation, so each person walks away with something of value.

Chapter 8: Effective Listening

There is something odd about the way we describe people whose professions revolve around communication. Writers *write*, painters *paint*, speakers *speak* and programmers *program*. All of these professions are recognized and defined by their output – the outward visible act of doing what they do.

This is sort of odd. It's actually not the physical act of painting that produces a great painting. Painting - applying ink or dye to paper - is something a machine can do. It's what is painted that makes a great painting. That comes from the artist's vision. Great speakers are renowned for what they say, their *in-sights*, not the act of making sounds with their tongues. Programming is the profession I'm most acquainted with. There's nothing worse than a programmer that thinks they can just write anything they like without first understanding what they have been asked to do. It really doesn't matter how much technical programming knowledge they have. If they can't listen, they're worse than useless.

Programming is a fun example, because it best proves this idea - *in a mathematical sense*. When writing a program, programmers often (well – in theory maybe) refer to a program specification. A specification is a description of what the program is supposed to do, usually in normal human language like English. The programmer's job is to take the English specification, and to translate it into a computer language like C, Java, etc. Specifications can be very detailed. In fact, a specification that is *complete* can be shown to be functionally identical to the same program in any other language – *Human or computer*. Of course, programmers are never handed a complete specification for the program they need to create. In fact, if they were given a complete specification – the job of the programmer might be completely redundant!

Instead, programmers are given rough impressions and vague ideas of what a program should do, and then need to fill in the gaps to arrive at a complete specification. It's this "filling in the gaps in the specification" that is the real work of programmers. They could do this through pure creativity, making up the answers to questions all by themselves in isolation, or they could do it by asking the right questions as needed to complete the program specification. A purely creative approach is fraught with dangers - it can miss requirements, overlook error conditions, and make assumptions that should have been handled. A good programmer needs to combine these two.

Unfortunately, most programmers would describe their jobs as driven by personal creativity, and completely overlook the requirement for communication. While it's true they need to be creative, it's not particularly pertinent. Like applying paint to a surface, that's *how* they do what they do. They use their creativity to solve a problem. *What* problem they solve (and if it's the right one), depends on how well they listened before they started applying their creativity. Serious problems arise if they failed to listen and misunderstood the problem.

The most effective communicators I know (and the best programmers) are also the best listeners I know. They are the people who are able to hone in on what other people are saying, what they need, and what their problems are. Furthermore, the best listeners are able to discern what others care about. The ability to relate to others and to listen to them carefully is far more important than the ability to speak or write clearly. For starters, effective listening is essential to learning. The more carefully you listen, the more efficiently you can gain new ideas. This is an essential business skill—it allows you to recognize opportunities and risks.

How does one become an effective listener? The biggest challenge to overcome, particularly for geeks like myself, is to actually make a real effort to listen. When you are knowledgeable about a particular subject, it's tempting to just push the conversation forward without actually listening to what the other participants have to say. That's a mistake. Even if you know a lot, there's always something more you can learn. And in order to understand who you're talking to, what they want, and what they know or don't know, you need to listen to them.

Asking Questions

The first step in becoming an effective listener is to become an *active* listener. To fully participate in a conversation with someone, you need to interact, and that means asking good questions and really thinking about the answers. Albert Lee's book *How to Meet the Queen* focuses on this subject with the premise that asking good questions is a key technique to achieve one's goals.

It helps to have a general framework of questions in your own mind to understand people you meet. In his book, Albert suggests you can understand almost anything better if you can come up with 6 "attributes" to characterize them. I like to paraphrase attributes as questions. So here are some questions I always try to ask myself when I meet someone in a business setting:

1. What values does this person really care about?

People have different values in the work place. Many developers I work with would likely carry on programming even if they weren't getting paid to do it. They care deeply about creating something. Others just want to get paid. Some sales people (the good ones) genuinely want to help their customers and see them succeed. Others just want to make a sale.

2. What are this person's cognitive biases and vested interests?

We've talked about cognitive bias and vested interests. When you walk into a room filled with people, some of them will be waiting there for you to stumble over. If you want to communicate with these people, you need to be able to navigate around sensitive topics without offending them and without contradicting something they believe very strongly.

3. Is this person an introvert or extrovert?

This is an important question to help you adjust how you are going to communicate with a person. Talking to extroverts and introverts usually requires changing the tone a little bit. With extroverts, I use more direct and assertive sentences. With introverts, I tone it down a bit, and use qualifying words more like "I think", "maybe" and "probably".

4. What does the listener not know?

This critical question can help solidify, in your own mind, what it is you need to communicate to someone so he or she understands you.

5. What does this person already know?

As we saw in Chapter 5, new ideas have to be built on something. If you are going to make your message understandable and believable, you need to connect into the ideas and beliefs already in your audience's head. Existing knowledge can lead to confusion if it seems to overlap or contradict your message. This is especially a danger in technology, because we tend to reuse terms over and over for new things.

6. What are this person's objectives?

In the coming chapters, we'll examine the subject of objectives in depth. Understanding a person's objectives in a conversation is the most immediate element of effective communication.

By starting with these six questions, you can build a fairly complete picture of who an audience is in a business setting. With that picture, you can tailor your message to reach the audience much more efficiently. Understanding who is in your audience is one of the two cornerstones of effective communication. In the next chapters, we'll explore the second corner stone that we'll refer to as *"the objective"*.

How do you listen to the audience when you are writing?

Actively listening to your audience is essential even if you are communicating with them through a written medium. When you are not engaged in a direct verbal conversation with someone then you obviously need to take a different approach to listening.

There are two things you can do to make sure you are readily listening to your audience. First, make sure you find out as much about it as possible. Spend time trying to figure out what information it has previously seen, or might have access to. If you are writing for a large audience, try to have a conversation with a small sample of people to get a sense of who they are and what they want. It's sometimes worthwhile to take a look at other written works that targeted the same audience to get a sense of what they focused on. You can ask similar questions to the audience regardless of if you are talking to it directly, or through another medium.

Second, wherever possible, seek feedback on what you've written from your audience. Check to see if your readers understood what you wrote, and most importantly, if they found it valuable. And remember if there are problems, you usually have a chance to go back and rewrite them for greater clarity. This isn't a bad thing; it's all part of respecting and understanding your audience.

Listening in a group

Sometimes the challenge in listening is recognizing what you *aren't* hearing from an audience. As I mentioned in Chapter 2, introverts are far less likely to be vocal with their points of view than extroverts. And extroverts tend to be people with high social confidence that naturally gravitate to the top of social ladders. This is why most organizations are led by extroverts. And why in discussions and meetings, extroverts easily overpower introverts. As research has shown, introverts are less likely to speak out in meetings and may even have slower reaction time than extroverts in dialogue. Our society values quick and witty speech, so slower thinkers have a hard time winning arguments against extroverts anytime there is contention. Introverts also may tend to avoid adversity, leading them to lose confidence in their convictions. It's perfectly reasonable to expect that in listening to a group, you will most clearly hear the views of the more extroverted, vocal members.

None of these tendencies of introverts suggest that they might have worse judgment than extroverts. Just because you can win an argument doesn't make you right. Quite the opposite – it's reasonable to expect that people who are slower to react and speak with *less* conviction may tend to have better judgment because they are *more* cautious and less confident. I'm not trying to suggest introverts are always right. There's no magic rule to guess who might have the right answer in a group. It could be the person with the most experience on a subject, or it could also be the opposite. The person with the least experience might have fresh and valuable insight. But confidence is no guarantee of correctness, so it's important to hear from everyone, not just those that are the quickest to speak (and with the loudest voices).

Managers dominate conversations far more than they should. Since a manager is more likely to be an extrovert than the people that work for him or her, conversation in a meeting is likely to be heavily skewed in favour of what the manager has to say, rather than what his or her employees have to say. Combined with the discrepancy in status, most managers can have a chilling effect on communication if they are not careful. This is a serious problem since successful businesses succeed by meeting the needs of their customers, and in most businesses, customers typically communicate with people who are *not* managers. It can create a form of blindness that allows the whims of leaders to set a company's course rather than solid business cases.

The solution is obviously to build an organization that listens to its own people. This can be hard to create. For an employee to challenge or question what his or her boss says (or the boss above, or the boss above that, and so on) he or she needs both courage and risk awareness. As we'll examine in Chapter 16, it's naïve to assume that a person in power is always going to be receptive to contrary ideas.

Managers and other leads, thus, have a challenging job. They must always be listening to themselves to make sure they are not drowning out the other voices of the people that work for them. They must also create the opportunity for everyone to be heard, sometimes against the natural tendencies of their reports. I've noticed that good Managers make a habit of prodding quiet members in a team to evoke their opinions. This creates (forces?) an opportunity to balance the conversation away from more dominate participants.

Cultural influences also play a large role in how a group behaves in a discussion. A friend of mine is tasked with travelling the world delivering training on our products. He's often commented on the troubles he has when teaching the class in Japan, because they have a very strong tendency to not ask questions during the class. His conclusion is that it's not socially acceptable in the group environment to be seen as ignorant. This is an issue, since he's delivering complicated technical content that requires clarification in the form of answers to questions. It's very inefficient because following the class, he has dozens of emails containing questions (usually the same questions) from the students. If they had only asked the question during the class, he could have addresses them immediately for the group.

A solution I propose in this situation is to make an alternate channel available that avoids the social barriers - for example, in this situation, by providing an anonymous chat group that allows participants to post questions during the class. That would allow students to pose questions as they think of them and then allow the instructor to respond to them during the class for everyone to hear.

Pulling Teeth

To take an active role in listening, sometimes it's necessary to go a step further and actively *evoke* someone's perspective with probing questions. One technique that is sometimes necessary in a technical conversation is to play dumb. If you ask questions that force a person to explain how something works, you can usually overcome their resistance to speaking up and providing the information on their own.

A slightly different technique is to use a structured list of questions that explore a topic and force someone to respond with specific information. This guides them through what they need to say for you to understand them.

As a last resort in extreme cases, I have even used obviously incorrect statements to *force* quiet introverts to respond and participate. This is a psychological trick that puts them in a position of power, giving them the security to speak out, while also pushing an emotional button by saying something they know is wrong.

Effective listening is skeptical listening

You might get the impression I'm suggesting everyone should have an equal say in all discussions or that all points of view are valuable or that you should just ask questions for the sake of asking questions. That's not the case at all. Questions should be asked so the answers can be examined skeptically. Part of active listening is applying critical thinking to what you are hearing - testing it to see if it is true, or if it falls apart under scrutiny, and asking for more details, examples or proof when necessary to judge its truth. Actively challenging an idea is usually the best way to flush out the reasons why it's correct.

You probably know the phrase: "The customer is always right". One of my roles has always been to work with customers to understand their needs. I'll be blunt – through my entire career, across multiple companies, I have always had favourite customers. Some are on the ball, organized and technically competent. And others are not. Some customers know exactly what they need and can effectively communicate them to me. Those are good people to work with. Others don't understand their own needs, or can't clearly express them. Working with them is challenging.

This doesn't mean you should react negatively to every answer you get when you ask a question to someone. It only means you should honestly and carefully consider what you are hearing as an active process. It's also a show of respect for the person you are listening to, demonstrating that you value their input enough to think about it.

Chapter Summary

- Effective listening is a critical skill in many professions. It's essential to understand your audience.
- Be prepared to listen to your audience. Have a framework of questions ready in your mind to help you model who your audience is. Think about who it is and what it is trying to accomplish.
- Seek feedback from your audience whenever you can to gauge how well you are communicating with it.
- Challenge what you hear. Get more details to ascertain why it's right or wrong.
- When necessary, evoke and probe to discover what someone is thinking using questions.
- Be aware of social roles or barriers that may prevent individuals in a group from speaking up, and mitigate them where possible.

Chapter 9: Plan to fail to avoid failing

You can't win all the time. There will be some audiences that are simply unreceptive to what you have to say to them. The best communicators know this and accept it. In fact, they expect it. I believe what makes some people truly gifted at communicating is the constructive way they react to failure, and their ability to persist in trying. Let's examine a few general ways communicating with an audience can fail, and how we can plan to overcome these failures.

Vested Interests

Vested interests are one obstacle that can make an audience unreachable. A vested interest is very similar to a cognitive bias, only they usually stem from a more conscious realization that the acceptance or rejection of a particular idea might be personally advantageous. They are very close to objectives, which is the subject of the next chapter. Objectives, however, in the context of communication are specific to a particular conversation. They are what the speaker or the audience wants to communicate or understand in that discussion. Vested interests are more general, and are not specific to a single conversation. They result from a person's general situation or world view; their identity.

Consider someone tasked with evaluating two products from competing software vendors. If that person happens to be an expert on one of the products, they will likely enjoy better job security if it is chosen. On the other hand, if a different product is chosen, and the person has no experience with it, his value to the organization might be decreased. So he has a vested interest in seeing that the product they know the best is chosen.

If you consider the position of members of the guild of computers from Vienna in 1500, it's easy to see why they might argue that common folk doing arithmetic on their own might be a bad idea. If everyone could do it for him or herself, there would be no need for professional computers! Human computers would be out of their jobs. Any arguments in favor of this new change (such as the benefits of eliminating the waste and inefficiency added to commerce by having guild members performing the business calculations) would be completely lost on them because it would not be in their interest. As it's been said, "It's impossible to convince someone of something when their livelihood relies on not believing it".

Another easy comparison could be made to those working in the recording industry or traditional publishing business. Making copies of musical recordings or printing large volumes of books used to be difficult. It used to require a huge physical infrastructure, which meant it needed the backing of investors. Wide distribution of books or records required a network with retailers. Marketing records or books required substantial spending. But all that is gone now. Since the digital age has arrived, the cost of copying music, books, and any form of information is trivial. Distribution cost is also trivial thanks to the internet. Marketing is the last and quickly falling value proposition traditional publishers have left, and social media is quickly undermining that. The friction of publishing something has disappeared, so almost anyone can do it. The traditional publishing businesses now lack a meaningful business model, and are thus likely doomed to disappear. But that doesn't mean they don't intend to fight to preserve the status quo using any means possible. They have a vested interest in arguing that these changes are bad, because they make their careers irrelevant. Every time an established business model is challenged, there will be people who will argue that the new change is bad, because of their interest vested in keeping things the way they are. This is unfortunate because it can slow the progress brought about from new ideas.

It's usually impossible to convince someone to hear you when they have a vested interest in not listening to you. The only solution to this problem is usually to go around the person. Instead of trying to change the mind of someone with the vested interest, change the minds of the people around him. At some point, he will buy into the idea out of peer pressure, lose credibility with the wider audience, or occasionally, try to convince you why your idea is wrong.

Leave a positive experience

Even when you can't find agreement with someone, it's important to try and leave the interaction with a positive feeling. Besides making the world a nicer place (which it does), there are strongly pragmatic reasons to do so. When your audience looks back on the exchange later on, it will associate what you've said with its feelings when you said it. If the tone of the conversation was negative and confrontational, then your audience will avoid thinking about it. If it was a positive and challenging experience, your audience will be drawn back to it. With time, your audience may even revisit some of the things you said that they disagreed with, and re-evaluate them, all because it felt good about talking to you.

Leave your message behind

Sometimes, even if an audience is receptive to what you have to say, there simply isn't enough time for the audience to absorb it. The message won't fit in its available channel capacity. In these situations, you should assume that you won't be able to communicate everything you'd like to. I often need to give training sessions on technical topics in my work. To be frank, people retain very little technical information from these classes. Technical facts are simply not absorbed well in a classroom format. People retain the same information much better when they look it up for themselves. So rather than focusing on directly communicating the facts, I try to provide the same material as a hand-out or as part of a reference, and then emphasize the importance of the reference. If listeners walk out of the room and forget everything I've said, except where to find that reference or with a hand out in their hand, the training can still be a success.

Any time you are giving a presentation, you should think about leaving your audience with printed material or web links that further communicate your message, especially where you need to relay any fine details. Written materials have an advantage over verbal communication. They usually enjoy a much higher channel capacity, since people usually seek them out when they want to know something in their own time.

Change the messenger, keep the message

Regardless of what you do, you still can't reach everyone. Even when you know you are right, and even if you are an effective and articulate communicator, there will always be some people who will not accept what you have to say. I encountered this early in my career. I had been acting as a DBA for an application team that was constantly encountering problems. The web server crashed every day and was constantly disconnecting from the database. The application team insisted that this was the database server's fault, not their application's. After the issues went on for a few weeks, they were noticed by upper management, and began to escalate. Bosses began to demand an explanation for the problems.

These issues weren't hard to find. There were some pretty obvious problems with the way the application was set up. To start, the network connection for the servers running the application (which were slow to start with – a modest 10Mbps) was shared with all the office workers in our building. Secretaries sending pictures of their cats and dogs would saturate the network, making it impossible for the application to reach the database. There were other obvious problems too, including some questionable decisions made by the application team. I quickly pointed out these obvious deficiencies, but, to my chagrin, was usually ignored. I should acknowledge that I was fairly young, opinionated and lacking in some social graces. No doubt these factors influenced how my co-workers listened to me. There were also no doubt occasions when I had pointed out problems that really weren't problems. So I probably had a mixed track record in the minds of my audience.

Enter the hero of our story. Driven to act, our section manager brought in an expert consultant, a slick and knowledgeable looking fellow named Cameron, or "Cameron 911" as my co-worker and I secretly quickly began to call him. You see, besides a professional demeanor, the most noticeable thing about Cameron was his impressive shiny and new Porsche 911. While only a few years older than us, Cameron clearly knew what he was doing in the consulting business.

I was anxious to see what brilliant insights Cameron would provide. He clearly must be an expert to charge the rates he did. After making the rounds to shake hands, he carefully listened to our boss explain the problems with the troubled web application. He nodded thoughtfully through this, jotting notes in his notebook, without saying much. After an hour or two, he came down and sat next to me and my co-worker.

"So guys, what do you think the problem is?" I was mildly surprised by this, since I had expected him to tell *us* what the problem was. Wasn't that what we were paying for?

"Well, to start with the application servers and database servers talk to each other over the office network, and that's already saturated", we explained. Once we got rolling, we listed off half a dozen issues we had already identified to our boss and the rest of the team on more than one occasion. Finally he said, "Ok, thanks, guys, that's really helpful". And off he went. After a week, we received his report, saying more or less exactly what we had discussed with him. I was sure that my boss would be irritated. After all, hadn't Cameron just told us everything we already knew? Instead, I was surprised when my boss began praising the report. It was, apparently, brilliant and insightful. And apparently well worth the forty thousand dollars we paid for it.

As you recall, there may be some neurological reasons to explain why the same message heard from someone else might be more believable and effective. There's an element of repetition to it, so the message will be more readily accepted. Other people might also have the benefit of a more positive association. New people, like external consultants, often seem very slick and knowledgeable; because they are novel, while the people you see every day, like your co-workers, seem more mundane and boring. Also, new people are not likely to come with any negative associations that naturally come up in working together on a daily basis. Sometimes people just need someone else to validate what you are saying to confirm it is true.

So, the solution in this situation was not necessarily to change the message, but to change the messenger. Go and find someone else to say what needs to be said. This could be someone who is more familiar, or even less familiar to the audience. Someone who might be either better trusted or just be more novel to your audience; or just someone that has a better car. And when this happens, don't take this personally. There's still value in what you have to say, even if not everyone will accept it directly from you. There's still a good chance that if your audience does believe your message after hearing it from someone else, they might, over time, remember that you also said the same thing.

Chapter Summary

- Expect that you won't always reach everyone you'd like to. Don't treat this as a defeat; plan for it to happen so you can switch methods of communicating.
- Recognise all people have vested interests that can direct what they say or hear. Avoid targeting someone with a vested interest who is not listening to your message. Instead convey your message to the people around him.
- Always try to keep the atmosphere in the room positive, because people will associate your message with the emotional state of the room.
- Leave your message behind with your audience by using other mediums, like written handouts, or links to online content.
- You can't reach all audiences. Sometimes someone else will have greater success saying the exact same things you have said. In these cases, go find that someone else.

Chapter 10: What's the point?

There is always a point to a conversation, but as always, it's very difficult to achieve a goal if you can't figure out exactly what it is first. That's why, to be an effective communicator, it's essential to be able to articulate your goal. Pursuing an *objective* is an imperative cornerstone of effective communication. But you must also realize that while you have an objective, your audience, also has objectives. The interaction between these two objectives can determine how productive the conversation is.

Shortly after I transitioned from pure engineering to technical pre-sales, Albert suggested I do a lunch-and-learn session for our parent company. These sessions are lunch time presentations, on any interesting topic, given for the entire company. Usually the topics were related in some way to our business, but occasionally the people would just give talks on travel experiences or other things of personal interest. Most importantly, they featured free pizza.

As a software developer with slightly introverted tendencies, public speaking was not my favorite activity. But since I was going to spend a lot of time presenting to customers, I figured I needed the practice. To my surprise, I did actually enjoy the experience. I discovered that the process of preparing and giving these presentations greatly helped me polish my public speaking skills. So over the next few years, I gave several more lunch-and-learns. Besides trying to provide some informative and educational entertainment for my co-workers, my primary objective in these talks was to practice my presentation skills. The people in the audience also had their own objectives. Some were genuinely interested in the topic of discussion. Others, I'm sure, simply wanted a break from their everyday work. But I'm sure the most popular objective was to eat the free pizza.

You might not give a lot of respect to "idle" objectives like entertainment or free pizza, especially in a work setting. You might believe that you should focus on serious objectives, like education or the latest business initiative. This is a big mistake, especially if you are trying to engage a group of geeks.

It's partially a mistake because it confuses your objectives with the audience's objectives. You should not assume they care about what you want to accomplish. It's also a mistake because "idle" objectives can also be the most engaging. If a presentation is slightly humorous or entertaining, you are guaranteed to have more positive feedback than if you cover the same topic in a dry and serious tone. People naturally want to play. Geeks especially like to play. I mentioned earlier that many of my co-workers that do software development would probably keep on coding even if they weren't paid to do it. Work *is* play for them.

Sometimes we overlook the objectives on both sides in a conversation when we really shouldn't. When in the audience, it's tempting to become passive participants who just absorb information without questioning what is being said. But unfortunately, if we do so, we are likely to gain nothing from the conversation.

People's objectives in a conversation are usually the immediate steps they want to achieve to further their interests. In some situations, when we question our objectives, the first ones that come to mind are not always honest. Consider a patient in a doctor's office, discussing her health problems with a doctor. Sometimes (usually when a person suspects she is sick), she just wants to hear the doctor say she is fine. She doesn't want to be *told* she is really sick, because she doesn't *want* to be sick. Patients can consequently sometimes downplay some symptoms when talking to their doctor. On the other hand, sometimes patients just want someone to talk to and listen sympathetically to them. Other people want to be told that they *have it bad.* Those patients can exaggerate symptoms to their doctors. Similarly, a salesperson can slant what they say; in fact anyone can slant what they say or hear to fulfill their true objectives.

Some people can also react in a conversation based on irrational attempts to justify the effects of framing and conditioning we talked about previously. If you like someone's appearance or how he speaks, you are automatically going to be more receptive to him. Finding value in what he says becomes your subconscious objective. If you don't like him however, subconsciously finding something wrong with what he says can also become your objective. Neither of these helps you if your goal is supposed to be objectively evaluating a speaker's message.

Occasionally, you might feel that you really don't have an objective to fulfill in a conversation. In these situations, it's inevitable that you're going to struggle to pay attention. Your mind will start to wander to things you do find interesting, or do care about. Honesty is sometimes (but not always) the best policy here to avoid wasting everyone's time. If you're not getting anything out of the conversation, you can try to steer it towards a topic you want to talk about. Or you can, as politely as possible, try to remove yourself from the conversation.

A Win-Win

In the previous chapter, we mentioned channel capacity as a limit to how much information a speaker could relay to an audience. The speed of the conversation and the length of the conversation are both factors that limited the channel capacity of an audience, (as is how much patience it has for listening to the speaker). In a conversation, the patience of participants is also going to be greatly affected by how much they feel their objectives are being met. If someone feels the conversation completely ignores what he wants to cover, he will likely have much less patience with it. If the conversation takes too long to address any of his objectives, his channel capacity goes way down. He becomes impatient, and his attention begins to drift. He may drop out of the conversation altogether before anyone can achieve their objectives.

Allowing everyone to meet his objectives while still attaining your own is not always easy. In the last chapter, we talked about communicating with a mixed audience. I did this often when presenting our technology to potential customers. Usually, there would be a fair number of technical people in the room, and one or two managers or executives. Invariably, there would be someone who would constantly ask questions. Sometimes they were good questions that improved the conversation. Sometimes they were bad questions that were off-topic or did not make sense. More times than not I suspect, the real motivation of the person asking all these questions was simply to be noticed. Everyone wants to appear knowledgeable and engaged when there's a boss around. And that's fine. I think the best way to keep the conversation moving is usually to accommodate these people and help them achieve their objective.

To hold an audience's attention then, a conversation must be collaboration between two parties. The speaker (who we'll assume is leading the conversation) has a challenging task. It's not enough just to achieve his or her objectives. The speaker needs to also achieve the objectives of the audience in order to hold their attention. In fact, when giving a long talk on a technical topic, I recommend trying to do so as explicitly as possible. It often helps to hold an audience's attention if you structure a conversation around any specific questions it has, while explicitly calling out the question. E.g. "Next, let's talk about your question regarding..." Again, to do this, it's critical to have an understanding of the audience, and what its objectives are.

Soliciting feedback in a conversation, even minor feedback, is a key element to effective communication. For example, when I'm presenting to an audience, I always try to take a pause and make eye contact with someone in the audience. Even this minor and non-verbal exchange gives me a sense of where that person is in understanding what I'm saying. Another, more explicit, way to do this is to stop after making an important point, and ask if the point is clear. This is also a great way to provide an opportunity for the audience to give valuable feedback on the direction of the conversation. Pausing and asking for confirmation after a point helps the speaker ensure he or she is reaching the audience's objectives while it works towards its own.

In a one-on-one conversation, it's even more important. Listening to a good conversation should be like watching a game of tennis. The speaker says something, the audience reacts, the speaker says something, and the audience reacts; back and forth. When this happens, it means both the speaker and audience are working in sync.

This is very much like a hand-shake in electronic

communication. When an electronic device like a computer is sending a very long message, it will often stop transmitting and send a signal that asks the receiver if it's receiving the message properly. This prevents the transmitter from wasting time if the transmission is not being received. It also provides a way to make sure the receiver can keep up with the transmission. If the transmitter is going too fast, then the receiver might miss part of the message.

Geeks often have trouble with this back-and-forth exchange in conversations. It's not unusual for geeks to drone on about a particular topic, ignoring the fact that the audience stopped listening to them long ago. I suspect this happens because geeks are very interested in the topic of the conversation, and often seize the opportunity to talk about it. It can also happen because when discussing a complex idea, a whole series of concepts might be tightly tied together. Breaking up this series of concepts into discrete understandable statements can be a difficult challenge. This can lead to a natural temptation to rush through the entire series of concepts in a single deluge. Unfortunately, this can leave the audience in the dust, or bore them right out of the conversation.

A Lose-Lose

There's usually some sort of trade-off between achieving your own objectives, and helping achieve the objectives of the person you are speaking with. We often refer to a conversation as an exchange, implying something is being traded between two parties. This is very accurate. A good conversation is an exchange that helps both parties achieve their objectives. Sometimes the objectives of both people line up, and there is a synergy between everyone participating. Sometimes the objectives of the participants are independent and unrelated. But discussion can still benefit everyone, as long as attention is paid to seeing that everyone gets what they need out of it.

Admittedly, there is sometimes a direct conflict between the objectives of people on two sides of a conversation. Consider a typical job interview. There is often a cliché question like "Why should we not hire you?" As Albert Lee mentions in *How to Meet the Queen* this is not a productive question. As he points out, it's not going to generate an honest response. I believe this is not productive since it puts the objectives of both parties in direct and irresolvable conflict. The interviewers want to solicit honest information from the question to objectively evaluate if they should or should not hire the interviewee. The interviewee on the other hand wants to craft an answer to portray himself as a good candidate for the job so he can get hired. The question has no good answer, because it gives the interviewers and interviewee very different objectives.

A friend of mine recently complained to me about the quality of technical white papers put out by high-tech companies. She was trying to evaluate a software product, and wanted to know what its limitations were, so she could determine if it was suitable for her purpose. Unfortunately, the "technical white paper" she downloaded contained almost no useful technical information, or even a concise description of the product. I sympathized with her frustration. Technical white papers produced by high-tech companies are almost always nothing more than glorified marketing material. These papers almost always portray a product in a positive light, and rarely mention limitations or drawbacks.

Regrettably, the technical content in these papers is often a race-to-the-bottom for companies that are competing. If a company does put out a candid technical paper with complete information about the suitability of a product, including the limitations, they may get trumped by a competitor that includes only positive descriptions in its marketing paper. Moreover, any limitations a company mentions could become fodder for competitors to attack it with. Ultimately, the objective of the company in producing these papers is to sell the product, so they write a paper with that sole purpose in mind. It's another example of a conflict of objectives. The reader wants hard information, the company wants positive spin. This direct conflict of objectives in the conversation almost always makes both sides lose. The conversation goes nowhere, and both sides leave without gaining anything.

Playing your own part

When an audience fails to consider the role or vested interests of a speaker, it fails to participate fully. Let me emphasize this; the issue is not that someone with a vested interest will present false things. However, to explore if something is true in a conversation, each side of the conversation might need to take the responsibility of playing a different role. You could compare a conversation that is trying to evaluate an idea like a court room case. If you have one side defending an idea, then you need another side prosecuting the idea. Someone needs to look for holes in the defendant's logic. So by ignoring the role of a speaker, the listener neglects his or her own role. There are two possible outcomes when this happens.

The first is that the speaker, if he or she cares enough, is forced to shoulder the responsibility of the listener. In my case, I had some strong motivation to avoid taking on customers that would not be happy in the long run. Besides having ethical qualms about it, I knew that it would make my life hell to have an unhappy customer. Small start-ups live or die on the enthusiastic support of their first customers. So I was occasionally stuck in an uncomfortable position; protecting customers from themselves, by trying to do their due diligence for them, and occasionally killing a sale. This was a task that was usually counter to immediate self-interest, because I had to stick my neck out to argue against making a sale and taking desperately needed revenue. It was in conflict with my job description as a sales person. It was also usually ineffective since I was put in a position of arguing against a customer who wanted to go ahead with our software.

The unfortunate, and probably more common outcome, is that the message of the speaker goes unchallenged and unexamined. This happens particularly in mass communication, like advertising, where conversations are more or less completely one-directional. For example, a television commercial is designed to get you to buy a product. They are not legally required to explain to you why you should not buy the product, except in some unusual cases like pharmaceuticals. And even in that case, the warnings about side effects are usually presented in a diminished volume or in fine print. It's understood in advertising that it's the audience's responsibility to think about what it sees in the ads, and exercise proper due diligence.

During my time in sales, I always found it frustrating when the prospective customers I visited failed to ask any probing questions or share any relevant concerns. As an employee for a struggling start-up in a sales position, my job was to inform, but also convince a potential customer to try our software. In conversations, I tried my best to do that job. On the other hand, doing the full due diligence to the customer's satisfaction, by asking good questions, and exploring any potential concerns, before trying the software was the customer's job. They are the ones that knew their particular requirements and challenges best. Unfortunately, some customers sat back and cruised through these discussions without raising any questions or concerns.

When listeners fail to think and challenge what they are hearing, there's usually a tendency to put the blame for the missed information on the speaker. Listeners might feel there were things they were not told that should have been said. What listeners usually fail to understand in these situations is that they might have had some responsibility in evoking the information they needed from the speaker. To avoid these situations, it's always important to think about what role the speaker is going to play based on their vested interest, and what role the listener needs to play in order to balance the conversation.

Chapter Summary

- Having a clear objective is essential to effective communication. It's helpful to frequently consider your objectives to keep them clear.
- Every participant in a conversation might have different objectives in a conversation. For the conversation to be really successful, it needs to address everyone's objectives.
- If you bore an audience by not meeting its objectives, it will stop paying attention to you.
- Asking for feedback in a conversation is a good way to calibrate what you are saying with the audience's objectives and ensure that you are meeting those goals.

- Asking for audience feedback also provides a way to gauge how well you are meeting your own objectives and if the audience understands what you are saying.
- Conversations must alternate back and forth at a regular frequency. If a conversation does not alternate back and forth, your audience has probably tuned you out.
- If the objectives of all the people in a conversation cannot be reconciled, they will all walk away having gained nothing from the exchange.
- Lead with your objective, and then follow with the explanation. Anticipate that your audience may make a decision long before you finish delivering your message.

Chapter 11: Noise

A common stumbling block for geeks is a failure to realize they need to have an objective to communicate and work towards in a conversation. Failing to recognize the need for a specific objective in a conversation can happen in a couple of different ways. As I have previously stated, geeks like to explore subjects and ideas. It's a natural inclination that comes with a curious and sharp mind. Often I'll be in a conversation with a geek, and he or she will go on a tangent without realizing it's off topic. Geeks may go through the details of one particular software function, or explain at length why something works the way it does and completely lose the objective of the conversation.

This problem is best explained with another borrowed concept from electronic communication. In electronics, when a signal is transmitted across a medium like a wire or radio waves in the air, there is always some amount of noise picked up by a receiver trying to draw out the transmitted message. Besides, the raw bandwidth, how much information can be transmitted (the channel capacity) is also limited by the amount of noise that is present. If there is a lot of noise in relation to the signal, very little information can be transmitted. The information gets drowned out by the noise. As the ratio of signal-to-noise increases, more information can be transmitted. As it decreases, less information can be transmitted.

In electronics, the signal might be a message encoded on a changing set of radio amplitudes of frequencies, or a pulse of light. Noise takes the form of random changes in the physical phenomena the signal is encoded in: a jump in the amplitude in a radio signal caused by distant lightning, a shift in the frequency of signal because of a faulty circuit, or the loss of a pulse of light because of a speck of dust in the way.

In a conversation, the speaker's message (set by the objectives in the conversation) is the signal, and is encoded in the words he or she says or write. Everything said that is relevant to the speaker's objective is part of the signal. Everything irrelevant to that message, like comments about the weather, confusing words, meandering observations or off-topic commentary is noise. When the audience is trying to figure out what the speaker is trying to say, it needs to be able to filter out all that noise, and pick out just the signal. This requires valuable brain power and effort, because it immediately doesn't know what message the speaker is trying to send.

Since geeks love to talk about technical subjects, they often wander in their message. They go on tangents, fill in unnecessary details. They will add points that are irrelevant. They simply say *too much*. This is because they are thinking about the whole subject of conversation, rather than focusing on their objective. They also tend to overlook the fact that the person they are talking to might not have a clue what they are trying to say. Geeks often assume even if they go down a rabbit hole, the audience will be able to distinguish that topic from the main topic. This sea of noise can easily drown out the speaker's signal, along with their objective.

Wandering aimlessly around a topic is not always a bad thing, if that's the purpose of the conversation. Sometimes it's fun just to have a casual conversation without focusing on one topic. But in these conversations, the point is to wander. When you have a job to do, and the conversation has an immediate objective, this is not ideal. In these cases, the speaker or the audience usually has a clear objective they want to achieve. It could be a question that needs to be answered, or an idea that needs to be communicated. In these cases not striving towards an objective makes it harder to get that job done.

If you find yourself going off topic, there are two ways to deal with the situation. The first is to stay focused and to ensure that you force yourself back on topic. If you have limited time with your audience, this is usually the best course of action. On the other hand, if you do have time to explore a side bar and your audience is willing to put up with you, then another good way to handle this situation is to explicitly say that's what you are doing. One might say, "Hey let's talk about this detail just for a minute". Similarly, sometimes you might want to talk a concept through before you continue in the conversation just to make sure you have got it correct. Again, the best way to handle this is to do it explicitly, by informing the other people in the conversation by saying something like, "give me a minute to verify exactly what this means". The common theme in both of these is explicitly stating what is going on so it's easy for the audience to pick up on what is going on.

As a listener in a conversation, there's no need to waste time constantly struggling to track what the speaker is saying when he is hard to follow. This doesn't help anyone, not the audience or the speaker. It's tempting to sit back quietly and let the conversation go on without saying anything, assuming that someone else is getting something of value out of it. We are often taught it is polite to listen quietly, but this is actually not true. When you sit back and stop trying to understand a speaker, what you are really doing is devaluing his time and your own.

A great way to keep a conversation on track and to make it easier for a listener to follow is for the listener to ask the speaker what topic she is currently discussing. What is the point she is trying to make? There's a social convention to not do this. It requires some courage on the part of the listener to admit he doesn't understand what the speaker's point is. It also requires some patience on the part of the speaker, because she may have assumed she was being very clear. The reality is that when an audience doesn't understand what the speaker is talking about, the blame lies on both parties, not just the audience. After all, it could be that the issue is not the audience's lack of understanding on a subject, but rather the speaker's ability to communicate that is failing.

I've explained that one of the most common ways to fail at achieving an objective in a conversation is to simply not understand exactly what the objective is. You might be surprised at how often this happens. I dread getting into a group discussion with someone when they say "*Let's all get together to talk about subject X*", without really defining what *specifically* we are going talk about with subject X. This is because I know at the end of the conversation there will be no real progress towards any particular goal. The conversation really had no goal to start with. Often the real point of these conversations is to answer the question, "I don't understand this subject, and can you help me understand it?" This is a good objective, and it is one that requires a certain amount of humility and courage to admit. The problem is that not acknowledging the objective works contrary to achieving it. If the audience does not acknowledge that it doesn't understand something, it misleads the speaker. It makes it more difficult for the speaker to understand and fill in what the audience doesn't know.

In the software industry where I work, another very common form of this problem is obvious in a lot of technical literature, like product user guides. There is a lack of clarity in this type of document because the people who write technical literature for software products are almost never the people who actually work on developing the software. In fact, it's not uncommon that the people who write the user guide of a software product have never even used the software they are writing about. Many technical writers typically work using design documentation for a software product, and start work on the documentation long before the actual software is finished. Design documentation, of course, is written to achieve a completely different objective than that of a user's guide. Furthermore, professional technical writers usually have no way to distinguish what is significant in what they write from what is useless filler. They lack the context to understand what they are reading, so they can't provide the right context for what they are writing. That's why many user guides are filled with small snippets of relevant information buried in piles of garbage. This observation would probably not surprise anyone, except perhaps some technical writers. Without a deep understanding of their subject, tech writers can't focus on a clear objective.

Sometimes we do have a clear idea of what our objective is, but have a hard time getting around to saying it. This could be because we know the audience might be sensitive, unreceptive or hostile to our objective. Providing constructive feedback to people when they don't want to hear it is a good example. In these situations, we can devote so much energy in cushioning what we are trying to say, that we fail to actually say it. Sometimes this can happen with mundane objectives as well, just because we fail to emphasize the main point of our message, or hide it in an obfuscated form. For example, using unnecessary negation in a sentence makes it hard to understand. Consider these two sentences:

The standby system will not be used, unless the active system fails.

The standby system will only be used if the active system fails.

Which do you think is clearer? Most people prefer the second, because it does not involve the unnecessary negative tense. It's much clearer and more direct, and so it's much easier to understand.

As Albert Lee, suggests in *How to Meet the Queen*, having a specific objective is essential to having an effective conversation. One of the best methods for doing so that I've borrowed from Albert, is to always ask questions. One of the most frequent questions I find myself asking on a daily basis is "What am I trying to say here?" I find that is an excellent filter to weed out irrelevant noise from the message I'm trying to communicate to an audience. Another (one that might be useful to technical writers everywhere) is "Was this conversation of any value to you?" or "Did this document help you in anyway?" These are essential questions that should be asked frequently if we want to gauge if what we are saying actually achieves our objectives.

Leading with a conclusion

You might remember being taught how to construct logical or mathematical arguments in school. You were likely taught to put the conclusion at the end of your argument, following all the points that support that conclusion. This is the natural order you would follow to *acquire* new information.

But when are trying to *communicate* information, the order is reversed. People need to understand the context and objective first, and then they evaluate each fact that supports it later. Writers often describe this arrangement as "The Writer's Pyramid", because the conclusion is at the top (or start) of the conversation, and all the details that support it follow.[10] Failing to follow this order, as many geeks

---

[10] "A difference in logic distinguishes the process by which writers acquire information and the reading process by which readers assess information. When business and technical analyst's problem solve, they

often do, leaves the audience feeling confused and impatient. It makes the speaker's point less apparent.

Leading with a conclusion is also important because your audience may decide whether or not they agree with it almost immediately (even if they don't do so consciously). Once it has made that decision, it can be very hard to change it. The audience can shift from listening to your message, to attacking your message in order to defend the decision they've already made about it.

The first few minutes of a presentation are consequently critical to making your point. If you recall, I mentioned that if you are in a business presentation and presenting to a CEO, you can expect to lose his or her attention in only a few minutes. If your objective is to gain his/her approval, you need to do it quickly. The technique for tackling this problem is to lead with your conclusion, and then follow up with the rationalization later.

Answer Questions

Another very common way geeks lose the point of a conversation is to not directly answer questions that are aimed at them. This is ironic; directly answering questions is a skill all school children are taught in grade school, but one that few adults seem to retain. When people fail to address questions directly, it's usually because they have become impatient and have jumped ahead of the person asking the question. They usually respond with a statement they feel relates to the question in some way. Unfortunately, geeks are often the only people who understand how their statement is related, because they haven't *communicated* that relation.

move from specific facts to larger concepts, reaching conclusions last. When readers attempt to understand the results of this work, they need to know the context or conclusions first, so they can evaluate each fact based on what they have been already told it will prove." - Writing Reports to Get Results: Quick, Effective Results Using the Pyramid Method by Ron S. Blicq and Lisa A. Moretto (Sep 6, 2001)

Consider this conversation:

Q: "Should we have steak for dinner tonight?"

A: "Today is Tuesday."

Does the answer make any sense? To an objective third party, clearly it would not. What does Tuesday have to do with having steak for dinner? The missing context in the answer makes it clear.

Q: "Should we have steak for dinner tonight?"

A: "Today is Tuesday." [...and we are going out with the Johnson's for dinner tonight at that Italian restaurant.]

Not directly answering questions is actually triple failure. By not making the connection back to the question, the answer becomes much harder or even impossible to understand. The questioner is left wondering what he or she is missing. In addition, the person asking the question is left with the feeling that he is being either ignored or talked down to. This naturally evokes a negative emotional response, which makes the conversation less pleasant. In work environments, direct questions are sometimes ignored by people because they don't feel they know the answer, and are hesitant to admit it. This is also a serious failure, since the question might be important, and not acknowledging that you don't know the answer will leave you in ignorance. Finally, it assumes that the person answering the question knows what information is really pertinent to the questioner. This is not necessarily the case. Have you ever had to drive to someone's house, and asked for the address, but got directions instead? If so, you can see the problem. People today use GPS to navigate, which is why they like to know the address of their destination. The GPS device provides the directions. Not everyone understands this however, which is why some still attempt to provide directions when asked for an address. Directions, of course, can be much harder to use than using a GPS, especially when you are driving by yourself (you either need to memorize them or try to read them as you are driving).[11]

---

[11] The obligatory XKCD reference: http://xkcd.com/783/. This is a book for Geeks after all.

In some discussions, it's natural for a single objective to break down into a whole series of sub-objectives. These sub-objectives are always interdependent. For example, if I want to explain to you how to use a piece of software, I might need to first explain what it's for, and then explain how it works, and finish off with what it can't do. There's an obvious order required to cover these topics. If I started by explaining what it can't do first, then you'd likely be fairly confused, because I hadn't yet explained what it was for. So getting the order right for these points or sub-objectives is extremely important. As we discussed in Chapter 3, the right order will ensure that the right context is provided to the audience to understand each point.

This process is essential when trying to cover a complex technical topic. Complex topics require filling in background context for the audience to understand the main point. In order to ensure the audience has the necessary background to understand a particular point, the speaker will usually need to follow a certain sequence in her topics, covering the background points first, and then building to her main points later.

The need for this order is why it can take a lot of thought to break a really complex topic down into a series of smaller points that can be delivered to an audience. Finding the best order to deliver these points is not always obvious. It's further complicated by the fact that the audience may be already familiar with some of them, and will not want to spend any time on them. They may however be anxious to get to the points they don't yet understand.

A common habit of really good public speakers is to always explicitly identify the upcoming topic before speaking about it. This gives the audience some additional clues on what they are about to say. That makes it much easier for the audience to understand what the speaker is getting at. When there are a series of points that need to be covered, providing an agenda or overview of topics the speaker is going to cover also helps quell the audience's urge to jump ahead to the particular points they want to hear, without skipping the background they might need to hear to fully understand it.

If the speaker doesn't provide this agenda, a listener in the audience is doing everyone a service by explicitly asking the speaker to lay out what they are presenting at that time, what they are going to cover next, or when they are going to get to a particular point. This is all great feedback for a speaker, because it gives them an immediate sense of what their audience understands and what they want to hear (in other words, what the audience's immediate objectives are).

Again, explicitly introducing what you are going to talk about has an immediate parallel in the electronic world. In the software world we might describe an agenda or title for a topic as "Metadata" (data about the data). In software, metadata might be used to decide how to check a block of data for errors, for example, to make sure it conforms to a set of rules based on what kind of data it's supposed to be. A block of human readable material, like this book for instance, should only contain letters and numbers, not random binary data.

Repeat after me, "Repetition helps"

Repetition also has an important role to play in making a key point clear to an audience. Besides helping the audience remember the point better, as we saw in chapter 3, repetition also makes an important point easier to distinguish. If you repeat the main point of your message enough times, almost all audiences will be able to pick it up. In public speaking, this works especially well if you can encapsulate the gist of your main objective into a simple and powerful statement that you can repeat throughout your presentation. In a format like this book, repeating the main points at the end of each chapter also serves the same purpose. It allows you, the reader, to revisit all the points made within each chapter to reinforce them and to ensure you did not miss them.

This also has a direct parallel in the electronic communication world. Sometimes communication signals are sent with redundant information, like the number of bits in the message. This information is redundant because if the message was transmitted correctly, the receiver would be able to count that information by itself. But by also transmitting it, the transmitter gives the receiver a way to double check that the received message matches the one that was transmitted, and was not confused or garbled in the transmission. Sometimes messages are sent with enough redundancy that even if there are a few mistakes in the message itself, they can be corrected without sending the whole message again.

As before however, there is a limit to how much repetition the audience can withstand before it tunes out the message. This is another reason why repeating a short simple phrase can produce a good effect. Short statements don't take much of the listener's time. Trying to repeat a long list of facts multiple times will usually produce a bad effect, because the listener has to sit through the repetition and will become annoyed. How much repetition is necessary and how much will be tolerated depends on the audience.

This again has nice parallel in electronic communication. Error checking and redundancy are great for transmitting signals across communication lines that are noisy. But when a signal is being sent across a communication medium that has no noise, redundancy and error checking are wastes of time. The transmitter could use that time to transmit more of the message instead of adding in redundant information.

All of these points are guided by the same general principle; make it easy for the audience to grasp the message. The speaker should send as clear a signal as possible about what they want to say, so there's no confusion between it and the noise.

Picking up your own signal

If you spend enough time in a role where you interact with technical people, you will occasional find yourself in a conversation that makes no sense. Sometimes people do not know what they are trying to say, or they say things that are contradictory. The (not) funny thing about this is how often they don't recognize that they make no sense at all.

As a solution architect, part of my job is to listen to a customer's technical requirements. I once heard this from a customer:

> *Customer: We need to have no latency in our data between our two database systems. The data must always be in sync on both.*
>
> *Myself: Ok, so the data must **always** be in sync?*
>
> *Customer: **Yes**. But we also need to be able to write the data to one system first, and then check it. So we will wait before we copy it to our second system.*
>
> *Myself: Ok….so the data must **not always** be in sync?*
> *Customer: **Yes**, exactly.*

These two statements from the customer were, of course, contradictory. You don't need to be a technical expert to realize that. Ironically, in this case the customer was a technical expert, but did not recognize the contradiction. It's tempting to assume the customer was just "stupid", but I don't believe this was the case. Obviously, part of the problem was that this person did not really know what he wanted. His objectives were not even clear to himself. To re-use our communication metaphor, there was a problem in the transmitter. The challenge in the conversation was that he did not acknowledge that he was not sure what he needed, which perhaps suggests he was not aware of the obvious contradiction in what he was asking for. The conversation was generally unproductive, and the root cause of the failure was that he had not taken the time to listen to himself. If he had been listening to himself, I'm sure he would have immediately realized that his requirements did not make any sense. We would then have focused on how to reconcile his requirements, rather than try to work with conflicting statements.

Again, it's not always a bad thing to enter a conversation without knowing exactly what you want out of it, or what you need from the other person. Speaking out loud with someone can be a great way to sort out complex ideas and test your own reasoning. It allows two people to tag team in examining ideas and synthesize them into a coherent whole. However, this usually only works when both sides of the conversation realize that is what is happening. And it *never* works when neither side of the conversation understands what is happening.

Losing the point

Sometimes geeks don't just wander around a subject. Sometimes they jump. Geeks are usually smart people, so they tend to be able to make connections that other people don't immediately see. When they are speaking on a topic, and they want to shift to a different related topic, they sometimes do so in sudden jumps, without the conversational device known as a segue. A segue joins different topics of the conversation by making it explicit how they connect. Without a clear segue, or at least an announcement of the end of the old topic and start of a new topic, audiences can be left completely confused. As Geeks change topics, the objective changes and the signal changes. Again, this situation is not always obvious to geeks, because they know what they are talking about. They might see a connection between the previous topic and the current topic that is not apparent to the audience.

Remember, the audience is always trying to hone in on the message that the speaker is trying to send to it. As the audience follows along, they will be working hard, building up a context in their mind to understand what the speaker is saying. A sudden topic change requires dropping that context and starting a new one. But the audience might not realize the topic changed, so they keep trying to make sense of what they are hearing in terms of the wrong context. Once the audience does realize the topic has changed (if the new topic is not explicitly identified) they need to devote some time and valuable brain power trying to figure out exactly what the speaker is now speaking about. There is always the possibility they might get this wrong. They could think that the speaker is now talking about X, when they are really talking about Y.

To borrow one more analogy from electronic communication, it's like a radio station that suddenly shifts its broadcast frequency. To someone listening, they suddenly hear static, and then must scan up and down the broadcast spectrum trying to find the station again.

The solution, as before, is to always be very clear about what topic the conversation is on. If the topic is going to change, it's a good idea to say it out loud. This not only lets the audience know that the subject is about to change, it helps them "close up" the previous subject in their mind, so they don't confuse it with content from the new subject. It also helps them frame the new conversation with a name ("We are now talking about X"), which helps them understand better.

Clearly stating when you are going to change the topic is also polite. By explicitly acknowledging the topic change, it gives the audience a chance to voice if they are ready to change topics. Listeners might want to ask a few more questions before moving on. Or they might want to choose a different topic to discuss next. All of these increase the value of the conversation to the audience.

Sign Posts

Rather than understanding a subject as a single complex whole, a geek can break it up into many different little subjects. I often picture these little subjects as places in my head. The challenge is that for a complex topic, there can be a lot of these little places. In a conversation, it's sometimes hard to figure out exactly where the speaker currently is, or where they intend to go next. When this happens it becomes extremely difficult to make sense of what a speaker is saying, because you're never sure if you have the right context.

The remedy, as before, is to be explicit. If the speaker verbalizes what they are talking about before they get into talking about it, it gives the audience a chance to "locate" them on a mental map of the overall subject. It's like adding a sign post to the conversation; "We are here". This is another form of metadata that make it simpler for a speaker's message to get through to their audience. Care should be given to provide enough context to avoid confusion with other similar sounding topics, just like one would give a full street address. This helps a lot in technical subjects, because different parts of a system often have the same names for things, just like different cities often have the same street names. If you say you are on Main Street, you first need to know if you talking about Main Street in Manhattan, Main Street in Los Angeles, or maybe Main Street in Albuquerque.[12]

Just like different regions in the world, different subject areas can sometimes use slightly different dialects for similar things. Sometimes they use completely different names for things that seem similar. Recognizing these differences requires first recognizing the subject. To be clear, it's important to use the right words that fit the subject. Using the wrong name for things will lead listeners to believe you are talking about something completely different.

For example, one of the software products I work with has a feature to raise an "alert" when something goes wrong in the environment it's running in. When an alert is raised, it usually doesn't mean anything is wrong with the software itself. Instead, it's the software reporting some problem. Occasionally, there is a bug in the software itself, and it will record an "error" in a log file. This software also has a set of specific states for things. One day a support person contacted me for help because he saw an "error" in a log file. After a confusing conversation, we eventually established what he saw was actually an *alert*, not an error. Since the two names are not interchangeable in this context and don't mean the same thing, using the wrong name caused confusion.

This is a common problem when non-technical people, or even technical people who are less familiar with a particular subject, are trying to discuss the subject. They might not always use the right names for things. Usually this is because of ignorance. Occasionally, it happens out of laziness. Even after being told, sometimes people like to use their own names for things, without realizing how much harder this makes it to understand what they are saying.

---

[12] On the other hand if you're on Peachtree, you're probably in Atlanta, where it seems all the streets are named "Peachtree". This apparently is to ensure that no one ever gets lost (you always know where you are, because you are always on *Peachtree*).

Chapter Summary

- Always lead with the conclusion—the main point you are trying to make.
- Always try to answer questions as directly as possible or you will confuse and alienate the person asking the question.
- Don't add unnecessary noise to a conversation. Know your objective and stick to it. If you want to go off topic, be very explicit about it.
- Announce what you want to talk about next. Use an agenda to explain what you're going to cover and when. This will help the audience understand what you are saying. When you have a specific objective, state it as clearly as possible. Don't jump randomly around a topic or you will confuse your audience.
- Avoid using negative tenses as they make the objective harder to understand.
- If you don't understand what point someone is trying to make, *ask*. It won't only help you; it will help everyone in the conversation.
- When you have a series of points to make, think carefully about their order to make sure you are presenting them in the best way possible. Explicitly state which points you are talking about as you come to them.
- If you are listening to a speaker and they don't provide an agenda, ask them what they are going to talk about.
- Listen to yourself! Make sure you are actually covering your objective and question whether you are truly making sense to your audience.

Chapter 12: Choosing the *right* medium for the message

The form that communication takes can also be used to achieve the objective of a speaker. As you've noticed from the end of every chapter in this book, there's a list of bullets that summarizes the main points of the chapter. This serves two purposes. First, it creates repetition, making it easier for the reader to recognize and retain points. Second, it does so in a very direct and low-noise way. Since these lists are short, they don't take a lot of time to process, much less than reading the chapter itself. So for clarity and brevity, they win. On the other hand, if this book were entirely written in bullet points, you would be very unlikely to read the entire text. They aren't very interesting on their own since they lack the details and explanations that are in the full text.

The medium through which you choose to communicate a message can have a big impact on how useful it is to your audience. But too often, people writing about technology related topics fail to think about which medium would best suit their objectives.

Technical References

As I mentioned before, software guides are almost always written as references. This means they are almost always *read* as references. A reader will typically reach for a reference when they have a specific question they need answered. They'll then search the reference for that topic, using old methods like a table of contents or index, or more typically using modern methods like a text search. This has some immediate implications. First, it's important that in providing information in a reference, the reader will not read the entire volume. Very few people read the entire dictionary (and if they do, they do so because it's unusual to do so).

Second, the ability to locate specific information is critical to any reference text. This might not seem like a difficult challenge, but in practice it is. In software guides, you'll often find that many search terms return no results, because the documentation writers and the software writers didn't stick to consistent terms. Other times you'll find that a search term is equally useless because it's used everywhere throughout a reference.

Fortunately, today we have a familiar, universally recognized solution to the indexing problem – Search engines. It'd been years since "goggling" has been accepted in the English language as a verb. Goggling has become our favorite method to locate information, and is usually our first instinct when facing a question. For many, goggling has become the only method of answering a question that is thought of. Ironically, many companies have been slow to clue in to this facet of the modern world, and make it more difficult to search their online documentation.

To make locating information easier, a better alternative to a monolithic reference is to use shorter articles that cover a more specific topic. Using a shorter format helps keep the topic clear. It also usually helps the reader locate the article and information within the article when they are looking for it. A shorter format also means much less "noise", since it can have a more specific topic.

Wikipages

Wiki pages are a great medium for providing searchable reference material. Wiki pages have the added advantage that they allow a community to easily contribute and update new information. Those are substantial benefits. They are also a relatively low-effort medium to communicate with, making them a natural choice for small teams to track tribal knowledge. Unfortunately, that can also be their downfall. While a wiki format usually encourages everyone to add information, but not to remove old stale information. The result is usually a handful of really useful pages buried in a pile of outdated junk.

Diagrams

Sometimes a picture is the best way to illustrate a particular subject. For example, a picture is often a great way to show the relationship between a small number of things. Different forms of communication also come with their own channel capacity limitations: the amount of information that can be conveyed using that method. I would not want to read more than one page of bullets. It would be just too boring. Similarly, pictures can usually only show one thing clearly. It's been said a picture says a thousand words, but for clarity, pictures should only attempt to deliver one main idea. If you attempt to show too many different ideas in a single picture or diagram it usually becomes a confusing jumble. So a skillful communicator will carefully choose the form of communication he or she thinks will best suit his/her message and objectives.

Technical Presentations

Technical presentations pose some interesting challenges. Complicated technical content can be hard to follow on paper, where the reader has the ability to read at their own pace and review as necessary. Delivering technical content as a presentation forces the audience to move at one pace. And it requires the audience to focus on what the speaker is saying, rather than what they are thinking. Both of these dramatically lower the channel capacity possible, limiting the depth of knowledge that can be delivered in a presentation. So it's important to carefully evaluate how much information you can reasonably deliver in a presentation. When I give technical presentations, I work from the assumption that no one will remember the specifics of anything I said. But they will remember that I said it, that there is something they need to know. Armed with that, they can go looking for the specifics in reference material.

Presentations also pose a problem because of a common confusion. In our modern age, a presentation has become synonymous with PowerPoint (or other some slide show format). It was not always this way – this is a recent development. Our modern association between slide decks and presentations has led to the incorrect assumption that the content of a presentation is a slide deck. It's not. The content in a presentation is what the speaker and audience discuss. The slide deck is just a bunch of pretty pictures the speaker uses to illustrate the content.

If you have any experience with presentations, you've probably heard advice to not fall in the trap of reading the text on your slides. Most people are aware of this, but few actually understand why. This is the reason – the slides are *not* the content. For an analogy, think of a comic book. Granted, pictures in a comic book are important. But remove the dialogue and you've likely removed the story, leaving a series of pictures that only *suggest* a story.

Mistaking a slideshow for a presentation usually leads to a *very* boring presentation. There's no experience more painful than listening to someone read their power point slides for an hour. If reading slides was all a presentation required, then no one would ever give presentations! We could all just stay at our desks and read the slide deck at our own pace. That would be more efficient use of time and more effective delivery (and would save the calories from those meeting room donuts).

That *a slide deck is not the content* is a concept that most that do presentations understand immediately, while other around them don't. Often following a presentation, I'm asked for copies of my slides. There are two frequent reasons for the request. The first is to re-use them in other presentations. Assuming the person asking understands the intended audience for the slides, that's usually okay. The other frequent reason is more of an issue. People often want to use my slide decks as reference material. This doesn't work, because the material they want, the information in the presentation I just provided, isn't in the deck. What they really need is a live recording of the conversation. Even that isn't ideal, because it captures what I said to a particular audience, in a particular way, at a point in time. Remove the content from the context, and it may no longer be effective. Sometimes, I'm asked by others to review the content before I present it (by looking at the slide deck). This is usually counterproductive. The slides usually don't give the reviewer a clear idea of what I'm going to *say* during the presentation. Some might suggest the entire presentation be scripted in the speaker's notes (within the slide deck). That is okay for the third grade - but it's not the way professional business presentations work. Speaker's notes are meant to be just that – notes for the speaker. Reciting speaker's notes is even worse than reading the slides.

So, why have a slide deck at all? There are some good reasons. The purpose of slides should be to illustrate or re-enforce your points. Occasionally even to capture the audience's attention with a beautiful graphic, or a shocking illustration. Visual stimuli helps hold people's attention. A slide deck also helps establish a hierarchical social framework, much like the Conch shell in "Lord of the Flies". In a meeting, the person with the PowerPoint is the one that gets to talk first. Finally, a slide deck also forces a presentation to have a high level structure - a defined order of execution for communicating ideas. Without the slide deck, it's too easy for the speaker and audience to get lost in discussing topics that they are not ready for.

Online videos

Closely related to presentations are online videos. Online videos are a popular format for just about every kind of information today. You can find online tutorials for every conceivable topic, from teaching a toddler to use a potty, to removing and cleaning the spark plugs in your car. As an amateur wood-worker and general handy man, I'm a big fan of online videos for those topics. It's really helpful to see how a professional would deal with a toilet repair, or a complicated cut on a table saw.

On the other hand, as an IT professional, I can't stand them. For computer related topics, the inability to follow exactly what a speaker typed in a video is incredibly frustrating. A good computer tutorial usually requires the ability for the audience to cut and paste commands from a text. A video doesn't provide that. The only strength of online videos in an IT environment is the appeal of laziness. I've often found that if I have content I want to ensure people see, the best way to get them to take time out for it is to record a short video presentation on the topic. It lowers the bar for those who are busy, and, if done right almost seems like an opportunity to take a break with some TV. Online videos are also a good way of capturing presentations and retaining them for new audiences, with the obvious limitation that they are no longer interactive.

Email

Even dusty ol' email counts as a communication medium (believe it or not!). Email has a number of serious disadvantages as a form of technical communication. First, everyone gets *way too much* email. Second, most email clients have very weak search and bookmarking abilities, making locating emails for referencing difficult. Third, some people simply don't read their email.

Email does have some advantages however. It does have a built in tracking system to make it obvious if content was sent to an individual. You might not know if they read it, but you know if they *should have* read it. Second, chains of emails are good for documenting and retaining conversations. You can always go back a week later, and check exactly what was said. Also, email makes it easy to start an impromptu conversation with a group of people at the same time. That's hard to do in any other medium. Finally – and this is a big one for technical conversations in the IT world – you can cut and paste from emails.

Social Media

Social media is pretty cool these days (or at least it was five years ago). It's become so commonly accepted, most IT companies are trying to remold their corporate communications around a social media model. Take my advice – *don't*.

Social media works for... wait for it... *social* groups. It's a great mass media tool for companies to market with. But corporations are not social groups on the inside. People at business might be social. And they might work in groups. Corporations they are not social groups.

Corporations do not allow you to casually begin and end relationships with others based on whims, likes or dislikes. Your coworkers are your coworkers because you all have related jobs to do, not because you thought it would be chill to hang out. The idea that people would randomly self-organize for communication in a business around social lines is highly defective.

As a technical thought leader in my organization, when I have technical knowledge or an important advisory to communicate to my group, I need to know I can reach everyone that is a stake holder. The company org-chart defines the group of people, not a chart of my local social circle. Relying on individuals to opt-in to that communication is just silly. It's simply not a reliable method for internal corporate communication. If you want to be an effective technical communicator, skip the social media, and leave it for family pictures, TV gossip, and funny pictures of cats.

Choosing a medium

Not all these forms of communication are eloquent. No one will confuse a list of bullet points to Shakespeare. Flow charts will not be mistaken for Rembrandts or Van Gogh's. Effective communication is usually about clarity, rather than eloquence. There are also differences in how effective some forms of communication are with particular people. Some people greatly prefer to read about a topic, whereas others respond much better to a verbal conversation. Direct verbal conversations have the large advantage of allowing "error" checking between both sides of the conversation. If one person in a conversation doesn't understand something, the other person can usually realize it, and solve the misunderstanding. You can't do that in writing. On the other hand, people read at their own pace, and can re-read something that is written as many times as they like until it becomes clear (or until they get bored).

The best medium is, of course, *all of them*. When covering a technical topic, an audience will typically need access to reference material to look things up, guides to step them through processes and a presentation to provide an overview of the content as a starting point.

Wiki pages provide an ideal way to wrap all this information together and provide it in a single, easily searchable and referenceable, spot for anyone looking for the content.

Chapter Summary

- Consider the best medium for your messages. Some things are better said with a picture, diagram or in writing. Use bullet lists and tables when appropriate to communicate.
- Think about how your audience is going to use the information you are providing, and pick a communication medium based on that.
- If you're producing a reference, make it easy to follow. References must be easily searchable.
- References are good for providing technical details, if the reader knows what they are looking for.
- Wikis fall apart when they become overfilled with too much old content.
- Email is hard to reference, but easy to trace.
- Technical presentations are limited in their channel capacity and can only deliver a small volume of technical details.
- You can't cut and paste from a video.
- Social media has no place in internal corporate communications.

Chapter 13: The Six Sins of Communication

So far we've talked about some theory behind effective communication, and I've pointed out a few specific issues that geeks normally struggle with. These challenges all stem from problems with communication techniques. Attitude also plays a critical role in the success or failure of a conversation. Many books on communication discuss how to develop a positive attitude. In "*How to Meet the Queen*", Albert Lee provides some excellent pointers on this subject for a general audience. Being a self-professed geek, and working with many geeks over the years has made me realize that geeks are usually challenged with a specific set of attitude pitfalls.

These six attitude problems can be described as the deadly sins of effective communication, Sloth, Fear, Haste, Anger, Vanity and Greed.

Overcoming these challenges can be hard, because they require real personal growth, rather than just utilizing a particular trick or technique. But they are also the most rewarding challenges to overcome, since they will not just benefit how you communicate, but in all aspects of your life. I certainly can't claim to have mastered and overcome all of these attitude problems myself. I struggle with several of them every time I try to communicate with another person. Fortunately, simply being aware of them goes a long way to help manage them.

Sloth

The number one obstacle in communication is without a doubt, failing to try to establish proper communication in the first place. This is not only the most common troublesome attitude in geeks; it's also the most detrimental. After all, if you don't actually want to communicate with others, then there's no way you can become an effective communicator.

Why would someone not make an effort to communicate with others when it's appropriate? The first obvious reason is that, as we've discussed, many geeks are introverts. Many are naturally shy people that find engaging with strangers in a conversation taxing and stressful. They would rather settle into their comfort zone, occupied by tasks that don't involve interacting with other people. I've noticed that in an IT environment, it can be very hard to convince a software developer that explaining what they are building, is just as important as building it. But it is, if end users don't understand the software, they will immediately call our help line, which costs us time and money, or they give up trying to use the software and ask for their money back.

Some geeks will even question the value of communicating their ideas to people who don't already understand them. They only want to talk to people who already understand what they have to say, and they honestly don't see why they should invest the effort in reaching out to someone who doesn't. They reason that if someone else does want to understand them, that person should make the effort to "come up to their level". If this is your position, you are bound to have a limited influence on the world around you. In recorded history, there are no great minds that didn't try to communicate their ideas.

Communication does take some skills, although most people don't consider the best way to convey a message. As anyone who has studied communication can tell you, effective communication comes from a skill set that needs to be developed independently of the subject that is communicated. For example, being gifted in advanced mathematics does not automatically make you a fantastic math teacher. In fact, it might have the exact opposite effect. If you want to be a good teacher, you need to study teaching. To be an effective communicator, you need to study communicating. This can be a catch-22; it's not necessarily obvious to someone who has not studied teaching or communication.

So geeks sometimes make a token effort at communicating, but often they are just fooling themselves. In a software company, you see many examples of this. Often our software developers will create internal notes that only other developers can read, and then assume that they have done all they need to "communicate" that information.

Sometimes the only people that know these notes exist are the ones who wrote them. In these situations they never question where the information needs to go, who needs it, when they might need it, or how they are going to find it. The developer fails to recognize the existence of a specific audience. They might have written it on toilet paper and flushed it down the drain, because the information will never reach anyone else.

There is a big difference between writing stuff down and communicating it via writing. Here's one rule of thumb to remember to help tell the difference: if you don't know who your audience is, you probably aren't communicating properly. Another rule: if you don't get any questions or feedback, what you wrote probably was never read by anyone. Even negative feedback is better than no feedback. At least what you wrote evoked some reaction, so it was not a complete loss.

Fortunately, countering this type of failure is easy. Effective communication is a lot like software development. When software developers write a program, they don't just finish writing it, and walk away. They run the program many times and test it in different situations. A good piece of documentation, or a presentation should be approached in exactly the same way. There needs to be some validation that the attempt at communicating actually worked. The easiest way to do this validation is to ask people in the audience if it was valuable. Did they understand the documentation? Did they enjoy the presentation? Get some sort of feedback to determine if you were successful at communicating your message.

To be fair, in a typical work environment, even if geeks are willing to devote the effort to effective communicating, they are rarely given the luxury of time to do so. Companies are always trying to move faster. Deadlines are always sooner than they should be. Businesses always rush, and attention spans are always short. For example, in my work place, the geeks I work with are software developers, and they spend their days writing software. That's their job. Writing documentation, like user guides, for the software they create is *not* in their job definition. Like almost all IT companies, we have a separate team of technical writers for that. This system doesn't always work that well. Technical writers need to rely on the software developers to tell them what to write. Unfortunately, the software developers are racing to meet their development goals, and don't have time to communicate with them. Without this teamwork, the result is usually really bad documentation (and typically a lot of it). The tech writers rarely have any insight into what they need to include, so they compensate by including everything they can.

There is, of course, a point when the software developers are supposed to review the documentation. But they almost always skim through it, reviewing for major factual errors, and completely ignore if the documentation has any value. They almost never review the purpose of the document. Consequently, most software documentation is useless. The people who wrote it don't understand what its objective should have been. To make things worse, most of software documentation is written *before* the software is done. So it's natural that the software does not always function the way that the documentation says it will. It would be nice if software developers were given a chance to write the documentation for their own products. But that would mean delaying the next release of the software. It might not always be wise for customer service, but most companies would rather have a poorly documented piece of completed software than a well-documented piece of uncompleted software. It would probably surprise most software companies to hear that their documentation is poor however, because they rarely solicit direct feedback from their customers about the quality of their documentation.

Fear

Even when motivated to share something with the world, most of us have a little voice inside that stops us. It's said that *"it's better to remain silent and be thought a fool, than to speak and to remove all doubt"*[13]. While, I know this is witty, I completely disagree. We live in an exciting world. There is a lot to learn. It is unfortunate that we place so much importance on always being right that it drives some people to fear speaking up.

---

[13] This quote is generally attributed to Abraham Lincoln

Speaking out on a topic, any topic, involves taking a risk. Any time you take a public stage, you are exposing yourself to scrutiny. That's the price you pay for challenging people to learn from what you have to say. It's inevitable that with this scrutiny, someone might find some errors in what you are saying. They may keep these errors in perspective, and still focus on the majority of your message, or they might exaggerate the importance of minor details to attack you. Another possibility is that you may be completely incorrect, having misunderstood what you are talking about. I think there's wisdom in realizing that regardless of whether we are right or wrong, the dialogue itself is intrinsically valuable. It creates an opportunity to evoke the truth that otherwise would not have happened. It allows someone to correct an error in understanding, and to share that correction with everyone else.

Making mistakes is not the end of the world, or even a bad thing. Smart people make mistakes all the time. Truly smart people acknowledge their errors and learn from them. They don't let the fear of making a mistake stop them from trying to share what they know. It takes both courage (because you risk losing the respect of people) and humility (because you must occasionally admit to yourself and others that you are sometimes wrong). It is nonetheless critical to someone trying to communicate effectively. If you make a mistake and tell people the wrong information, they will receive the wrong information. It might become much harder for them to integrate the rest of what you are saying because the incorrect information will throw them off the correct trail of your message.

This is especially important to remember when you are delivering a presentation or talk to a large group. Even the most experienced and knowledgeable public speakers will occasionally make mistakes. It might be the reversal of a series of words, or confusing the details of one technical topic with another. Verbal flubs will happen. It's nothing to be ashamed of, or even to dwell on. The best way to handle these is to acknowledge them explicitly, correct them, and then move on.

Often when I'm speaking on a topic at work, I'm conversing with an audience that has two parts. The majority is usually a large group that knows almost nothing about what I'm talking about. And there are usually one or two individuals who know more about the subject than I do. This can be an awkward situation. I'm always asking *"Do I know enough?"* and *"Are the experts going to shoot me down?"* It's easy to lose confidence, so there's a fact I always try to focus on. On any given subject, there may be someone who knows more than me – but they aren't the person talking. Someone has to take the risk and open a dialogue or there will be no discussion and our knowledge will stagnate.

Haste

There is no doubt that effectively communicating with an audience can be a task that is both intensive and exhausting. Everyone has a limited amount of time and patience. At some point, you just want the person you are trying to communicate with to *get it*, so you can get on with the rest of your life. In a work environment, you might expect a co-worker to be able to pick up and understand what you are saying. If they are competent, it shouldn't require jumping through hoops to help them understand the same concepts you do. And there are always other time pressures. Taking the time to cover a subject in depth always takes time; time that could otherwise be spent *getting stuff done*.

In your social life, you may feel you should not have to work that hard to be understood by the people around you. You are who you are, and others should make an effort if they want to know you. I entirely sympathize with these feelings, and am prone to them myself. In my job, I often need to repeat the same message to people several times. This is extra frustrating because I often do it with groups of people (usually in the context of training). And then later I usually need to repeat the same information with people on an individual basis, even though I knew I'd already presented to them in a group. I sometimes catch myself wondering - *Did they completely ignore me the first time?* Repetition does help the audience understand and retain, but it can be very taxing on the speaker.

It's extremely easy to get burnt out when you are trying to help someone else understand something. It's hard not to focus on how many times you feel you've repeated the same message. Indulging in these feelings of frustration is self-defeating however. If your aim is to effectively communicate with someone and give them information they need, you sometimes need to suck it up and try it one more time. Allowing your feelings of frustration to surface simply makes the task at hand more difficult. People are extremely sensitive to attitude shifts in the speaker and their perception of your frustration will affect how they perceive your message.

Part of this haste stems from the fact that we often overlook how valuable and productive the act of communicating is. We minimize it, so we can focus on other things, but we shouldn't. If one person understands the information you present, he or she can produce something of value with it. If many people understand your information, many people can produce something of value. This is too often overlooked.

It's also wrong to assume that if someone does not immediately understand what you are saying, the blame lies on her. You should always consider the possibility that the blame is, in fact, yours. Consider that you may not be communicating clearly, or that you are not making your message easy to understand. You should, therefore, extend just as much patience to the person you are trying to talk to as you would like her to extend to you.

Everyone has limits though. Communicating with people is work. Just like with a physical form of work you need to take breaks. So if after making a serious and sincere effort to convey an idea to someone, you might reach a point when you find you are running out of patience. If you're an introvert like me, you might need to carve off some quiet time to recharge your emotional batteries before continuing. If you are an extrovert, you might find switching topics just as relaxing. But take some form of a break to allow yourself time to recuperate. This will also give you an excellent opportunity to evaluate if there is some alternate way to communicate what you are trying to say.

Sometimes, geeks are impatient even when the audience is fairly on the ball. When people get excited about an idea they really like, they tend to speed up. They stop focusing on communicating their subject, and start thinking about the entire scope of the subject itself. Rather than moving at a pace the audience can follow, they start going too fast for the audience to follow. In this situation, slowing down for the audience can be very frustrating for the speaker. But it is both courteous and essential.

Anger

As we discussed in chapter 1, the fact that we have a term for people like geeks implies that we are marginalized. Even if attitudes are evolving, we're not yet at the point where society is unprejudiced towards people who are a little bit different. Geeky school kids are still picked on. Technical people are still less likely to become leaders in business or politics. Science and technology are not yet "cool". We still have a long way to go.

As with any group that faces marginalization, it's natural that a certain level of hostility and prejudice will develop. I myself, had a very bad impression of sales people and business executives (at least until I was forced into a sales position). I felt they did not respect us technical people or what we had to contribute. The business world appeared to be an extension of high school drama, with clear lines drawn between the cool kids, jocks and cheerleaders, and the geeks in glasses. After my transition into sales, there were many situations that confirmed this view. I recall silently swallowing insult and anger when an executive in our high-tech start-up one day said "Oh, we could just outsource all this technical stuff and save money. We can have a dozen egg-heads for half the cost." It was extremely hard not to view this person in a negative light after that comment. It was also extremely tempting just to write him off and avoid further discussions with him. The unfortunate reality was however, that he did play an important role in our company. His opinion was important because it did impact the future of our company and everyone in it. Reacting in anger, while difficult to avoid, would simply undermine the argument that our technical people were professional and valuable.

When marginalized, it's hard not to react with hostility. For many geeks, self-isolation is the first instinct. When they feel they can't make themselves heard, they stop talking. They avoid conversations altogether and try to wall themselves off. This instinct is extremely self-defeating. It's one reason why geeks lack influence in society. They become comfortable with being marginalized and stop trying to influence others.

Around the time I had the aforementioned awkward conversation with the executive in my company, I became aware of some prejudicial feelings from my fellow geeks. I noticed their automatic assumption was that anyone in sales must not know what they are talking about. To be fair, they had just as bad an attitude towards non-technical people as some of the non-technical people had towards them. Some geeks assumed that being a business person meant taking advantage of people. They also believed that those in business had no insight into what we should be developing or working towards together.

So how do you break this chain of bad attitudes? Without respectful dialogue, these negative attitudes between technical people and non-technical will persist. It's unfair, but it's almost always the "insulted groups" that have the responsibility of correcting an attitude problem. They will need to help those who delivered the insult to understand why it was wrong. Respect in a business organization needs to start somewhere. Change won't start with the party in ignorance. And confronting and correcting negative attitudes towards geeks is critical, for the benefit of everyone, not just us.

Bad attitudes towards technical people in a technical organization are usually lethal to the business. You can't bite the hand that feeds you and then expect to get fed. Geeks need to try to talk to non-geeks, even when they are being marginalized. It's the only way to stop prejudice. Turning the other cheek, and persisting in working with someone in spite of their bad attitude, is not just a noble sentiment, it's a survival strategy. At the same time, ignorance and disrespectful attitudes must be confronted and corrected. If they aren't, they eventually poison the relationship between geeks and non-geeks.

Vanity

Vanity is a common failing of many geeks that negatively impacts their communication skills in a few different ways. We've already touched on the topic of "Dumbing it down" in regards to the channel capacity of the audience in Chapter 7. Many Geeks do not want to lower themselves to try and express an idea to someone who doesn't already understand it. The natural implication of this attitude is that the Geek is smarter because he or she knows something the audience doesn't. They are too important, in their own minds, to waste time with lesser minds.

To be honest, this is straightforward arrogance. It's too bad for the audience, because it misses out on what the geek could have contributed to its understanding of the world. But the person it hurts the most is the geek. What the geek is really doing by refusing "to lower" him or herself is becoming irrelevant to everyone else. His or her high esteem is usually limited to him or herself. This is why many self-confident geeks find themselves pigeon-holed in technical roles in business, with no real voice on how the business is run.

It's easy to see this sort of arrogance in the software world. If you use free or open source, you may have had occasion to try and seek help on an online discussion forum. While there are many helpful individuals in these forums who are ready to answer basic questions, there can also be individuals that have a negative "RTFM" (Read the F******* manual) attitude. This attitude is poisonous and silly for two reasons. It antagonizes the person looking for help. But more importantly, it's illogical. In today's age of Google and the web, getting access to manuals, when they exist, is trivial. It's highly unlikely that anyone would ask a question without first trying to answer the question themselves using an online manual, and a search engine.[14] The most likely problem is that the manual either doesn't exist, or it doesn't contain the required information, or it fails to communicate the information in an effective manner.

---

[14] http://developers.slashdot.org/story/12/09/30/2112230/wtfm-write-the-freaking-manual

158

Many people also don't realize that *no one* truly *reads* a manual. Manuals are references; a long collection or encyclopedia of factual information. As with a dictionary or encyclopedia, you do not consult sections of a manual that won't give you the information you want. Manuals are *referenced*, not read. People open them looking for specific factual information. They almost never start from the first page and read all of them to the last page. And even if they did, they would fail to retain all the information in the manual. This is due to channel capacity again - there is too much information in a manual for a reader to remember it all. The key to a good manual is making it easy to search for more information on a specific topic. They are rarely useful if you don't first know what you are looking for.

Here's a final form of vanity to consider; failing to recognize or admit when you are wrong or ignorant. This is, admittedly, a hard thing to do. We all want to be considered "smart", and smart people are people who are often right…right? Our culture is geared to value people who are always correct. We feel we always need to be "in the know", rather than acknowledge that we are often ignorant. As we discussed in the sin of fear, it's tempting to avoid taking the risk of appearing ignorant by admitting a mistake. Vanity is really the flip side of insecurity. But someone who realizes they made a mistake, and then acknowledges it is far wiser than someone that realizes they were incorrect and stays silent to protect their image.

Geeks often really struggle with not knowing something. Many geeks understand themselves as smart people, so to face a situation where they don't know all the answers can be painful. It can call into question their self-identify and self-worth. So many times, when faced with a subject they know little about, geeks will intentionally remain silent. The admission, "I don't know", is often very hard to pull out of a geek. This should not be the case. Not knowing something is not a bad thing, it's something that should be celebrated. All understanding starts with questions and all questions start with realizing there is something you don't know.

So, to a geek, not knowing something should be the beginning of a rewarding journey… but it's often not. Talking with some geeks on a subject they don't know anything about can be genuinely annoying. The burden of always appearing to have some insight on all subjects can produce some genuinely irrational and silly discussions. For some reason, some geeks feel that defending their status as smart people requires them to be authorities on all subjects.

Desiring to always appear knowledgeable is essentially a form of vanity. Arrogance is also a form of vanity, as is refusing to acknowledge when we've made a mistake. All of these should be avoided. But as sins, I think they are pretty forgivable. What I find most disturbing is the sin of greed.

Greed

The monopolization of knowledge is greed. There are some geeks who don't communicate what they know, specifically because they want to be the only ones that know it. Knowledge is a form of power, and by retaining knowledge and not passing it on, they are attempting to retain control over the people around them. It's an attempt to artificially inflate their own importance. This might occur when someone intentionally leaves a process or procedure undocumented so that only they know how to do it. It can also happen when someone secrets away information about the bosses or customer's opinions, so only they know how to please them.

The first reason this bothers me is that knowledge doesn't belong to any one person. As I mentioned earlier, there are many examples throughout history of ideas that had occurred to great minds at the same time. This strongly argues that these ideas were emergent, and really came *through* these people, but not necessarily *from* them. I make no claim of the ideas in this book. I'm lucky enough to have a good set of mentors and teachers that exposed me to these ideas, some of which I've internalized to produce this book. I can give credit to them, and they in turn can give credit to the people that taught them, and so on.

Secondly, any attempt to withhold information from others is a callous, selfish and anti-social act. Work like engineering is inherently based on social interaction between peers. Greed tears at the very social fabric that is necessary to get the job done.

In a work place, informational greed can be very disruptive. I have fortunately only seen this a few times. I believe it is a rare sin among geeks, who are generally inclined towards cooperation rather than dominance. But it does occasionally occur when people are too personally ambitious, leading to confusion, misunderstanding, and wasting valuable time. People who attempt to withhold information from their colleagues are not team players. They are ultimately working against the greater good of the organization.

It's not uncommon when an individual does this that it becomes apparent to someone else. As Richard Stallman, the founder of the FSF software movement once famously said "Information wants to be free". When someone does stumble on this *monopolized knowledge* and shares it with the world, there is a good chance the connection will be made back to the person that tried to withhold it, to question either why they didn't know about it, or why they didn't share it. Greed is remarkably foolish. In the cases I've seen this happen, the culprits are often incredulous. While they usually will not be able to explain why they didn't share the information with anyone else, they always insist that they knew it first. This leaves the question open as to whether their sin is arrogance, sloth, or greed...or perhaps all three.

Chapter Summary

- Attitude is extremely important in communication, and communicating effectively requires making an effort.
- Communicating is a valuable and productive activity, and deserves time to be dedicated to it. Make a sincere attempt to communicate with others.
- Communicating with others does require courage. It exposes you to personal risk from public scrutiny. But it is also a public service that everyone benefits from.
- Communicating is hard work. Take a break (in your own way) when you need to. Don't let your frustration seep into a conversation with your audience.

- Set an appropriate pace, and stick to it. Don't let your excitement, or impatience set the pace of a conversation. Conversations should take as long as necessary.
- Try to validate that you are actually communicating effectively. Test if your audience is getting your message.
- Recognize that becoming proficient at communicating requires developing some communication skills. Being knowledgeable on a particular topic does not automatically give you the ability to communicate that topic effectively.
- Don't react in anger to ignorance. It will undermine your ability to communicate why something is wrong or disrespectful. Confront ignorance with respect, and then work on knowledge acquisition.
- Don't take yourself too seriously. Don't assume you are smarter than your audience because you know something it doesn't.
- If you realize you are wrong, explicitly say you are wrong. If you think you are right, consider the possibility you are wrong. If you don't know something, say it. Only fools think they know everything.
- Consider that the knowledge you have may not actually belong to you. You have an obligation to pass it on. Intentionally withholding information is anti-social. Intentionally withholding information is an act usually doomed to fail. Information wants to be free, and will eventually find a way to come out.

Chapter 14: Perspectives on truth

In the beginning of this book, I raised a question about whether the goal of effective communication was to inform or influence, and suggested that they are actually one and the same. Informing an audience on a particular topic affects their thinking, their decisions, and in some cases, their understanding of the world. There are no passive "ideas", because everything we believe or disbelieve is linked together by neural connections in our brains. Since everything we say has an effect on other people, it is reasonable to ask, *are we having a good effect, or a bad effect?*

This is both a practical and philosophical question. We've actually already partially explored part of the practical side of this question. In a conversation, both sides will have a set of objectives they want to accomplish. If they can both accomplish them, then the conversation is probably going to be viewed as a success, and therefore "good". But besides achieving their short-term objectives, an ethical person will want to ensure what they are saying in a conversation is genuinely true. They have an unspoken objective that what they say and what they really believe should be consistent. This greater objective is usually one that is shared by both parties in the conversation. An ethical speaker will want to tell the truth, because their audience wants to hear the truth.

Even an unethical person will worry about telling the truth, if they are clever. Few people realize that being capable of lying really is a remarkable ability. This is because lies come with an incredible burden of consistency that makes them very frail in the long run. A clever unethical person will reasonably fear the negative consequences that might result if they tell a lie that is later exposed.

So there are both ethical and practical reasons to strive for honesty when you are communicating. You might therefore assume that being completely honest is trivial. All you have to do is only say everything that you know is true. Easy, right? Well, not so fast.

As I've mentioned, I started out as a technical person in a technical role (software development). And in that role, as a purely technical person, I had pretty deep confidence in the truth of most of the things I said. I strived to be not just completely honest, but complete, in what I said. When someone asked me a question, I would try to provide as much information as possible (sometimes *too much*), just in case the questioner needed it.

Then I was forced into a technical sales role, walking the line between engineering and sales. All of a sudden, the world got a lot more complicated. On my first sales trip, I began to realize that the strategy of being completely honest and forthcoming was not a workable strategy. At our first customer presentation, I tried starting with a list all of the things our software could not do. This satisfied my personal objective of telling the truth. Unfortunately, it left the bewildered potential customer with no option but to say *no* to trying our software. I had spent the entire time listing the reasons not to, and I hadn't provided them any compelling reason to try it. Obviously, this was a loss for my more immediate personal objective of keeping our software start-up in business. But it was also a serious loss for the customer. He was looking for a solution for a pressing problem, which our software could have addressed. By not providing them with a solid argument for trying the software, I was denying them their objective as well.

I was not fulfilling my role in the conversation with the customer. Our conversation was like a metaphorical kangaroo court with only a prosecutor and no defense attorney. Striving for honesty was also ultimately a zero-sum game in a practical sense, because by not making a strong case for trying our software, the customer tried to use a competing product from another software vendor that was much less concerned with its limitations.

As my experience with sales grew, I discovered to my surprise, that this wasn't actually the heart of the issue. The biggest issue in being completely honest was not the *honesty* part, it was the *complete* part. Every time I tried to educate someone on all the considerations and background knowledge they should know in order to make an informed decision, I'd find they were completely overwhelmed and confused. They rejected what I was saying, not because they disagreed with it, but because they could not understand it. They couldn't follow the details, or integrate what I was saying into a coherent whole. I exceeded their channel capacity. The complete truth was simply too much information for anyone to digest.

So how can we reconcile the desire to be both honest and complete with the restrictions that effective communication techniques require? If we are hung up on hearing complete and absolute truth in every conversation, we're going to be pretty dissatisfied. So the first step is to look closely at how we perceive the notion of truth in what we hear. Here are three perspectives.

Right/Wrong

I'm not unique in trying to be an honest person. Most people who identify themselves as geeks would also identify themselves as people that value honesty. It's probably not the first thing you think of when you think of the geek stereotype, but besides having an affinity for technical subjects and science fiction shows, geeks tend to be actively moral people. I contend that geeks tend to question the morality of things around them, and have an instinct to frame the world in terms of "right" and "wrong".

If you accept that most geeks were the school kids that did well in school, and gravitated to science and mathematics, this makes perfect sense. The way subjects like science and math are taught in schools strongly favors simple blank and white interpretations of truth. Tests in science and math are usually graded with simple assessments of "Right" and "Wrong". It is natural geeks might pick up a tendency to view the world in simple terms of "Right" and "Wrong". Mathematics is indeed unique in that there is indeed a "Right" answer to a specific question. It's a one-off though; Scientists, mathematicians and philosophers have debated and explored how this differs from the "real" world that surrounds us for thousands of years. Mathematics is definitely a part of the underpinnings of the universe, but scientific method is built on the foundation that there is no way to deductively disprove a theory without making observations of the universe. Science values predictions of things not yet seen, even if they turn out to be wrong. Science *likes* mistakes. A good scientist shouldn't feel bad when he is wrong. He just moves on to the next theory knowing that he has made some progress. This attitude is why science is always improving. Over time, it provides us with better, more *accurate* and complete models of the universe.

Non-scientists often don't get this positive outlook on mistakes. In fact, scientists don't always get this positive outlook on mistakes. Remember the discussion of Newton's law of gravity? I once heard a remark from someone that it was "wrong". You could argue this is true. Although Newton's law of gravity can be used to explain the behavior of almost all objects here on earth, and in our solar system, it's not perfect. When it's applied to planet Mercury, it seems to be slightly "wrong". Mercury is deep enough in the gravity well of the Sun that the effects of Einstein's theory of relativity comes into play. However, as previously explained, Newton's Law of Gravity is not "Wrong", it's just incomplete. It's not a model of gravity that works in all situations, only most of our everyday situations. It doesn't work with Mercury because Mercury is moving fast enough that the effects of relativity become measurable. Newton's laws aren't accurate in this context. You need to use Einstein's theory of relativity to explain its motions, which comes with a cost.

Einstein's models require a lot more math than Newton's simple law of gravity does. Any grade 7 student can comfortably master Newton's law sufficiently to explain how fast an apple will be traveling when it's dropped from a certain height. Doing the same thing with Einstein's equations will produce an almost identical result (unless you are say, dropping the apple into a black hole), but with enough mathematics to make first year university students struggle.

This is why we keep Newton's law of gravity around; even though we know it's not as accurate as Einstein's relativity in some situations. It's less work, and we like simplicity. Similarly, if we can frame the world in simple terms, like right and wrong, it becomes a simpler place to navigate.

Nevertheless, the real world is filled with nuance. Earlier in this book, I used a survey that offered a choice between keeping $30 or gambling for $50. I noticed a difference in the responses I received.

One person pointed out that they do not gamble out of principal, and that was the basis for their decision. Another said that they felt lucky, and could use the $50. The geeks, on the other hand, tended to offer explanations for their responses that showed why one response was preferable. They seemed more likely to believe that there *was* a right answer, even though the question did not suggest there was one. They perhaps interpreted the question as a math problem, and were hoping to get a check mark from their teacher in lieu of the $30. But there was no "right" answer, simply a personal choice.

Right/Wrong to Good/Evil and Smart and Stupid

If you start off with a tendency to view the world in terms of "Right" and "Wrong", it's a small and natural progression to start framing moral questions in terms of "Good" and "Evil" or "Truth" and "Lie". This is perhaps why many Geeks also harbor a moral model of the world that is anchored in these absolute terms, and why they are quick to judge what others say based on them.

Google understands this. Their corporate motto "Don't be evil" is targeted specifically at geeks. As a high-tech company, they've always appreciated the importance of cultivating the respect and interest of the geek community. They understand the long term influence geeks have on technology, and the "Don't be evil" motto specifically tries to position Google in the good books of geeks everywhere, so Google will remain a favorite player in our high tech world. In 2013, the Reputation Institute, a global private consulting firm based in New York, ranked international companies based on their reputations by surveying 55,000 people. Google came in at number 4 in the list. Another survey done by the Harris Poll group showed similar results, with Google also coming in at number 4 in a list of top corporate reputations. I spoke to quite a few of my geek colleagues on how they felt about Google. Most generally view Google and its motto with at least a small amount of respect. All of them said they would trust Google more than Microsoft, Apple, Intel or Amazon, which suggests to me that Google has mostly succeeded, at least so far, in creating the image they desire.

I also asked a few colleagues in sales and marketing about how they felt about Google's "Don't be evil" motto. It didn't seem to register any reaction at all. They tended to be much more subjective in their moralistic outlook. "What's evil?" one sales person I talked to remarked (which is actually a valid and moral question). "Oh, it's a great tag line" commented another, without realizing I was actually asking if she *believed* it.

I've noticed other differences that further explain why geeks and sales people distrust and dislike each other. There is a funny thing about most geeks I know who do software development. Most of them want to be well paid, but not really because they want a lot of money. They want to be well paid because they want to know they are respected and valued. Most of them would likely continue on programming even if they weren't paid to do so. On the other hand, sales people are usually directly motivated by compensation (on a literal if not personal level). A typical sales person has a specific quota he needs to sell. When they make that quota, he gets the majority of his income. If he doesn't make the quota, he doesn't get his full income. This wouldn't work well with most geeks. As a geek, the idea that work would be motivated simply by the promise of a financial reward always struck me as slightly *distasteful*.

So, do geeks secretly yearn for a morally righteous world where complex situations would be resolved in nice clear conclusions? Well, consider the science fiction franchise Star Trek. It's undoubtedly very popular with most of the geek crowd. It's lasted over *47 years*. That's a long time for a show about the future. The future it started with in 1966 has been overrun a little bit by the present. Besides being a space opera, a drama set in a future setting, the best description I've heard of Star Trek (particularly the original series), is that it's essentially a weekly episodic morality play. Each week the crew of the Starship Enterprise explores new cultures or situations that inevitably raise troubling moral issues. And, through the course of the show, the moral issue is examined and then almost always resolved in some satisfying way. Here's the problem though: "Good" or "Evil" is a not a practical way to comprehend the world. And real moral questions are rarely wrapped up with clear and satisfying conclusions. Like the question of gambling the $50 or keeping the $30, there is often, in reality, no clear answer.

Geeks are not always comfortable with this uncertainty. But here's an uncomfortable observation, taken from *Super Freakonomics*, of all the terrorists in the 9/11 attack on the World Trade Center, the most common profession of the terrorists was that of engineer. This is surprising, and doesn't necessarily fit our imagined idea of terrorists. There are two obvious explanations. Terrorists might be more likely to be engineers because of their technical competence. That is certainly a reasonable explanation. Or terrorists might be more likely to be engineers because of their preference for a simplistic and absolute moral outlook. I believe the latter explanation is definitely haunting. It's easy to imagine terrorists recruiting someone with technical skills to support or contribute assistance to an attack. But you would assume these people, being in a support role, would want to take a back seat, and let some other psychopath take the glory. These engineers were the terrorists on the planes. They didn't just want to contribute to an act of terror, they wanted to be the main actors. It's safe to say: consciously choosing to kill oneself for a given cause requires radical moral conviction. People who have a *black or white* outlook on life are more likely to develop more radicalized convictions than others. Some engineers may thus be more prone to develop such convictions than non-engineers.

Terrorists are a dramatic example, but there are much more common examples in mundane everyday life. Anyone who works in IT long will know that silly differences in technology can blow up into melodramatic and long lasting disagreements. And most geeks, including myself, have a tendency to assume we inhabit a moral high ground. We have a tendency to view the actions of other, "less noble" people, like those in sales or management, with suspicion.

The danger behind seeing the world as "Good" and "Evil" is that these are empty words, devoid of any meaning by themselves. They are almost always used to *avoid* thinking about a moral question. They make the world appear much simpler than it really is. This is not to say that there aren't moral extremes called "Good" or "Evil". It's just that those words are moral arguments in themselves. They should apply to actions *after* careful consideration and judgment. They cannot be allowed to form cognitive biases that interfere with how we judge the world.

Fortunately, I believe that most geeks today are actually cautious and careful with the terms "Good" and "Evil". After all, religions and other moral frameworks have framed ethical questions in these terms for thousands of years. Hopefully, the average person today is fairly ethically savvy in comparison to those in the past and is able to critically question and judge for themselves moral issues without short-circuited prejudiced conclusions. Unfortunately, there is a new "Good" and "Evil" that has taken its place in the minds of Geeks. I believe that for geeks, "Smart" and "Stupid" has become the new "Good" and "Evil".

When you've worked in the IT industry long enough, you begin to appreciate the incredible effect of history on the present. It's sometimes fascinating to look at a piece of technology and wonder, why it is the way it is. When the present is not that desirable, it's easy to react in a negative way, and describe it as "stupid", rather than think about why it is the way it is. Computer programming, like all forms of engineering, requires evaluating trade-offs between different options. There are always pros and cons to almost every design decision. There are always influences like time, money, stress and emotion that greatly affect human actions but that are always forgotten after the fact. Choices are always made based on what was believed at the time they were made. Finally, decisions are always linked together in a chain, one leading to the next in a series of choices and consequences. But most people, including geeks, rarely think in these terms; we generally focus on the way things are right now, not how they came to be. When the present situation doesn't suit what we'd like it to be, we're dissatisfied, and react negatively.

I've seen this countless times in software development. It typically happens when a junior programmer digs into an old piece of software, and cannot make sense of it. In my first job, I had the unique experience of working on some software that was older than I was. Some of the code I worked on had been written at a time when programming approaches and concepts were different than those that I had learned, so making sense of that old code was a real challenge. One day I was debugging a piece of FORTRAN77 code. I simply could not make sense of how it was doing what it was doing. After staring at it for days, I threw up my hands in defeat, and asked an older programmer in my department for help. He looked at it for less than a minute, and said "Oh, that's a syntax error. You have a space between those words. FORTRAN doesn't recognize spaces." This blew my mind - I couldn't understand why a language would not recognize spaces. *What a stupid language,* I thought to myself. My older friend thought this was hilarious. As he explained, the code had originally been entered using punch cards, and "There are no spaces in punch cards!" My reaction to dismiss the language as "stupid", was misplaced. The way it worked had made perfect sense at the time it was used. But I didn't understand that context, so it was hardly fair to dismiss it as "stupid". That code had, after all, been working fairly well since before I was born.

A more useful perspective – Accuracy and Precision

I've used the words accuracy and precision a few times now. Recall that, in science, accuracy is usually meant to describe how "correct" a reading is. Experiments are expected to produce some fluke results. An experiment that produces the same result 9 times out of ten is said to have an accuracy of 90%. And precision describes how detailed the reading is. The finer the measurement, the higher the precision.

These are also extremely useful terms to describe communication. If a statement is generally correct, and fits most circumstances, it can be described as *accurate*. Obviously, it's desirable to be accurate when communicating, because then everything you say should be correct. And if a statement is very detailed, it can also be viewed as precise.

As we discussed in the last chapter, many geeks have trouble balancing the need for both accuracy and precision. They often mistake lack of one for the other. Of these two, accuracy is a requirement, but precision needs to be varied based on who you are talking to, so you don't exceed their channel capacity. When a speaker determines how much information she can provide to a particular audience, it's the precision of the message she needs to limit. There is simply not enough time to provide all the details on every subject. The trick is selecting enough relevant details that the message is still useful, while still being general enough that it remains accurate.

Accuracy and precision provide a much more useful perspective on the truthfulness of a statement than 'Right' or 'Wrong'. Rather than attempting to simplify the world into the single dimension of either "Right" or "Wrong", it provides a *two* dimensional perspective that recognizes the limitations of communication. It implies that if you aren't satisfied with the level of detail in a conversation, then your next step should be a second conversation with greater precision, rather than making a snap judgment.

Chapter Summary

- There are trade-offs made in order to communicate effectively with an audience that has a limited channel capacity. However, a speaker should never be condescending towards his or her audience.
- Many geeks tend to evaluate the truth of what they hear in simple terms of right and wrong, which leads to moral prejudgements and oversimplifications like "good" and "evil" or "smart" and "stupid".
- It is easy for these moral absolutes to turn into cognitive biases that interfere with our ability to listen.
- It's more useful to judge the truth of a statement in terms of accuracy (how correct it is), and precision (how detailed it is).
- The precision of information in a conversation should be tailored to the needs of the audience to avoid over or underwhelming them.

Chapter 15: Telling the Truth

Here are four typical approaches to communication you'll encounter, each with varying levels of accuracy and precision. Two of them are good styles, but with trade-offs that need to be recognized and in some cases mitigated. And two of them are bad styles that should be avoided. They inevitably lead to problems that risk the credibility of the speaker.

The Whole Truth

The first approach is the one most natural to most geeks; to tell the whole and complete truth on a particular topic with complete openness and transparency. A speaker striving to use this approach tries to provide both high accuracy and high precision. Unfortunately, it's generally why many people find talking to geeks annoying.

In theory, always telling the whole truth sounds like a good thing. Don't we wish everyone spoke with complete openness and honesty all the time? But as we now know, it's incredibly difficult to effectively communicate a very detailed message to an arbitrary audience. The precision of the message needs to be tailored specifically to an audience to fit both its attention span and what they are able to absorb. You can easily overwhelm an audience with too much detail.

The technique to mitigate this failure is to vary the precision of the message appropriately, and be selective about what details are relevant to the audience. Since the audience may have limited knowledge of the topic, it's the speaker's responsibility to judge what to include or exclude in the message for listeners.

Furthermore, the inclusion of too much detail will typically make the discussion erratic and sometimes cause it to get lost in details. If the speaker has a concrete objective he needs to achieve, this approach doesn't work well. For example, in the context of a sales call with a potential customer, someone needs to explain why the customer might want to evaluate or buy a given product. If the entire discussion is spent on explaining technical details of the product, the more general point of why the product might be useful will be drowned out.

I think the best way to mitigate this problem is to, if possible, separate out technical details into a second conversation, after the immediate short term objectives have been met (such as getting a customer to evaluate a product). This helps in a few ways. First, it allows you to "*put your best foot forward*", and create a positive first impression. You articulate your objective and avoid too much technical detail. Then later in the conversation, you can be more open in discussion, with both higher accuracy and precision. You may only want to do this with a more selective audience (for example, only the other technical people), that will be better equipped for a more detailed discussion.

Putting the best foot forward

Just like it sounds, the second useful approach to communicating involves leading with the most positive parts of your message. It means picking out both the most relevant and compelling points that support a particular objective, and conveying them in the most efficient way possible to your target audience.

The core of this approach is to develop an "elevator pitch". Imagine you are in an elevator with someone you want to convince to buy something. You only have about 30 seconds to talk to her before you reach your floor. What are you going to say? What are the most relevant and compelling points of your message? If you can create an elevator pitch that conveys the core of your message, it's usually easy to build it out into a conversation of any almost length, by adding in selective details.

This approach is suitable when you have a specific objective that involves influencing someone. It allows you to focus on achieving your immediate objective without becoming distracted by everything you know on a subject. It also avoids what is described as "leading with your warts". This is a typical failure by geeks when they aim to be completely open and honest. If they are tasked with drawing someone towards a particular objective, like evaluating a software product, they sometimes get sidetracked. Instead of explaining what the product can do, they might actually spend all their time explaining what the product can't do.

There are a few pitfalls with "the best foot forward" approach to be cautious of. First, it assumes that the person you are influencing will take responsibility for assessing what he needs to know, and will ask for more detail when appropriate. When this doesn't happen, the result could be a bad decision on the part of the audience. The audience might not think about the reasons why it should not do something, and later blame you for not telling it.

Although evaluating what the speaker says is the audience's responsibility, the speaker can choose to switch modes and lead his audience to ask him or her relevant questions. Or alternatively, the speaker can integrate the aforementioned "The Whole Truth" approach into his/her discussion to make sure that the audience is completely informed on the subject. This combination is powerful because it allows evaluating the potential benefits in the first part (*Putting one's best foot forward*), and understanding any drawbacks or challenges in the second part (*The Whole Truth*).

There's a second potential pitfall with the "Putting your best foot forward" approach. When are working as a team with other people to communicate a message, the other people working with you need to understand that is what you are doing. If you are putting your best foot forward, you are filtering out some negative points and focusing on the positive ones to put a positive spin on your message. This should only be done once. Unfortunately, what sometimes happens is that other people will repeat the same information they heard from you and then also try to add a positive spin. They may leave out details that you thought were relevant and required. Carefully qualified statements may turn into carelessly unqualified statements. When this happens both precision and accuracy drop quickly.

When I was in sales, I noted this happening countless times. If

I said: "Our software supports *most* clients.", then later on I would hear a sales person saying "Our software supports *all* clients". If I said "For a *typical* application the overhead is 15%", later I would hear our sales people say "The application overhead is 15%". In these cases, I had carefully constructed a statement that was accurate, but not too precise, in order to place it in a positive light. Trying to make the statement even more positive made it simply untrue.

This pitfall can be mitigated by clearly telling your audience what your objective is. While this is generally effective, don't expect it to always find an easy reception. In internal discussions with other colleagues, I get a lot of push back when I'm being completely honest with them about some technical topic, when they need to later position the same information in a positive light. Some would prefer to just hear something they can repeat without actually thinking about it. Unfortunately, this doesn't work. They need to tailor the information to make it relevant to their audience; it's their responsibility to understand and re-position the message. To fully understand the information, they need to hear an unbiased version of it. Only then can they manage the positive spin themselves so it remains accurate.

Combining the "whole truth" and "best foot forward" approaches works well both in verbal conversations and in written documentation. In documentation, it's helpful to be able to easily link together documents so it's easy to switch between content that aims to be general and content that aims to be very detailed. Marketing documentation, for example, should always provide links to technical documentation for readers who need more complete information. And technical documentation should be kept relatively clear of marketing spin. Not doing these two things will simply annoy and frustrate people trying to learn about a topic.

Little white lies

To be fair, putting your best foot forward is sometimes like walking a tight rope in a circus, while the audience throws things at you. In essence, it requires leading with the most positive points of your message, and delaying the negative points. There is sometimes a pressure, both from your own objectives and the audience's objectives to make statements that you are not sure are true. This creates a temptation to go a step further than simply putting a positive spin on your message by changing or altering minor details with "little white lies". I would describe this as an approach to communicating that stems from a conscious or unconscious decision to deviate from just trying to position things in a positive light, to being creative with the truth.

Little white lies are, of course, minor things that are not quite true, but you believe are *probably* inconsequential. Consider this situation. You're selling a product for a high-tech start-up. Your engineering manager has promised you that the next release of the product next month will include a new feature. Your slightly irrational customer tells you that they can't even consider the product unless it has this feature, and they need to make a decision now. However, you know that the customer will take two months to actually do the paper work to complete the purchase, and another 4 months to begin using the product. So that's 6 months away, and your next release is in 1 month. It's a safe bet that by the time they actually use it, the product will have the feature they need. Right?

In situations like this it's normal to be tempted to obscure the truth a little bit. One might, in this example, be tempted to claim that the new feature is actually available now. It's not technically true, since it's in the next release, but that will (should) be available very soon. So it's *almost* true. Certainly, the gap between it being false and it becoming true seems small. It's worth considering how we perceive this gap between true and false changes in this example as the timeline changes. What if the next software release was not available for seven months? Clearly, it would be false to say the new feature was in the software already, since the customer would be ready to use it in six months. What if it was only one week away? Does that change the situation? It's a pretty safe bet that by the time the customer uses the software the feature will already be there.

These situations are so tempting because of the perceived inconsequential nature of the white lie. In the example, the feature will be available soon, and before the customer is ready for it, so it's reasonable to say that the difference between it being available now and in a month does not actually have any real consequence. It's also tempting when the speaker is highly motivated to achieve his/her objectives in the conversation by telling the audience what it wants to hear.

 Regardless of the motivation, there are a few serious dangers in opening this door even a little. Without fail, something will happen to make the statement in question more false than true. For example, in the aforementioned scenario, product releases are always late. If the product release date is pushed back, then a claim that the feature is already in the product is false. The gap between what is true and almost true always tends to get bigger with time. A second danger is that the audience might do some fact checking and notice the gap between what was said and what is currently true. Even if this gap is small, the perception of the gap might undermine the rest of the speaker's message. Since people judge truth based on consistency, any inconsistencies suggest that the message is not true. And as a general rule, if changing an insignificant detail does make a difference, it probably is not a little detail. Lies also tend to travel. As Mark Twain once observed, "A lie can get halfway around the world before the truth can even get its boots on." Once out it the wild, even little lies can take on a life of their own.

 Finally, as we've discussed before, it takes a lot of effort to lie well. Distinguishing what is almost true and what is not, requires a deep knowledge of a subject, much deeper than simply sticking to what is undeniably true. The previous example of when a new feature will be available in an upcoming software release requires insight into timelines, staffing levels, capabilities and even vacation time. And that's just to cover what is actually possible to know. It doesn't begin to address the unknowable questions of what might go wrong. If you are not certain how large the divergence is between what you are saying and what you know to be true, there is a good chance what you are saying might turn out to be completely wrong.

Bullshit

Bullshit is a vulgar, but highly effective word for things which are obviously not true. To confess, of these four approaches to communicating, I actually find it the most intellectually fascinating. This is because many people unintentionally do it, but almost no one does it intentionally. It's extremely rare that anyone would go into a conversation with the intention to say something that they know is not true. People, in general are actually very honest. You could be an optimist and attribute this to something positive about human nature, or simply chalk it up to how difficult it is to tell a lie that isn't obvious. But if few people intentionally set out to bullshit, *why do they end up doing it anyway?*

I think there are two common sources of bullshit in a technical conversation. The first is confirmation bias. This is the tendency of people to selectively emphasize things that favor their objective. Notice that this sounds a lot like "Putting the best foot forward", only instead of presenting that positive spin on a message to someone else, you are presenting it to yourself and believing it. This sometimes takes the form of overestimating how well a topic is understood or how certain a fact is. In other words, misreading the accuracy of what you believe. It's tempting to believe that when something *almost* makes sense except for a few little details that it must make sense. It's easy to assume the details that don't fit must be irrelevant. That's one possible explanation. An alternate explanation is that the details that don't fit actually are significant and your understanding of the subject might be fundamentally wrong in some way.

Confirmation bias can also take the form of favoring desirable assumptions. When you need something to be true to succeed, it's tempting to assume it must be true. For example, if you have 5 days to complete some work, you might assume it's *possible* to complete your work in 5 days. But the world doesn't work like that. Things don't always work out the way we'd like. While this is something probably most of us realize individually, if you've worked in business long enough you might also recognize that it's something that contributes to many failures. From a different perspective, confirmation bias is a failure to recognize and mitigate risk.

Bullshit also creeps in as a message that is repeated and retold by other people. We've already discussed this in the second approach, "Putting your best foot forward". When I said something that was imprecise but accurate, it was sometimes repeated and modified to be precise and inaccurate.

The classic childhood game of *broken telephone* also illustrates this. The game starts off with a group of children in a circle. The first child is given a message to whisper to the next. That child in turn whispers the message to the next child, and so on. When the message reaches the last child in the circle, they say it out loud. The point of the game is that as each child relays the message, they inevitably introduce errors. They change words, rearrange them, or even add things to the message. When it arrives at the end of the circle, it's always (and usually humorously) wrong. This is true with children as well as adults. Geeks often discuss technical topics, where it's a significant problem. The more complicated a message is, the more likely it is to be miscommunicated. As it's relayed from person to person, there will be some details that will be left out intentionally and some that will be changed or left out unintentionally. The farther the message gets from someone that can correct it, the more errors it accumulates.

How should we react when we hear a person say something that is obviously not right? You could start by considering the possibility that they are not doing it intentionally. The speaker may genuinely believe what they are saying, or he may only be trying to seem like he does. This could happen for a number of reasons. He might be afraid to admit that he isn't entirely sure about what he is saying, or might be afraid of losing the confidence of people around him. He might genuinely not understand the difference between what he is saying (which is inaccurate), and something he previously heard that was accurate. He may be trying to put a positive spin on his message, without realizing he's gone too far.

This happens a lot in high-tech companies, and other organizations, because the consumers of the information (the audience) are often far removed from the origins of the information (*behind the scenes where the geeks work*). Engineering departments will typically write documentation that will be read and simplified for a wider audience by a pre-sales technical person. What they write will be typically read by a sales person, who will create "sales literature". The sales literature will typically be read by a marketing person to produce marketing material. At each step, each person will typically try to add a positive spin on the message, to "Put their best foot forward". The result is often something that is far from accurate.

This also explains why there is so much material that is clearly recognizable as *BS* to many people, even though no one intends to produce it. Individual people are very smart. They recognize when something makes sense and when it does not. They can easily distinguish something that is plausible from BS. But groups of people are usually not nearly as smart. When groups of people get together, social dynamics take over. These do not always work in favor of clarity or consistency. Work is divided by necessity; individuals in the group vie for rank and attention is given based on who is the most persuasive, rather than who is the most intelligent.

While an individual can improve his/her communication skills to become an effective communicator, it's extremely difficult for a large organization to develop the same skills as a group. This is why organizations usually fail miserably when they need to communicate complex messages. Many of the skills discussed in this book, like questioning cognitive biases, listening to an audience or picking up your own signal, are skills based on self-introspection. This is something that groups of people are less capable of exercising when they act as a whole. Individuals in a group might be good at introspection, but that does not mean the group is. If someone in a group has an insight about how to better communicate an idea to an external audience, he or she first needs to convince his or her group of it. That is usually a challenge, since it requires the rest of the group to realize something it did not. Groups usually do not learn new things as easily as individuals do.

One tactic for dealing with this is to eliminate group dynamics when faced with a communication problem. Select one person who is an effective communicator and allow him or her the freedom to craft an effective message. But be careful to choose the right person. It needs to be someone with a solid understanding of the message.

For individuals, there are easy ways to avoid being a source of inaccurate information. Before you say something, you should always do a reality check. How do you know what you are saying is accurate? How sure are you? If you are repeating something you heard, are you sure you fully understand it?

The moral here is to be cautious in assessing what you know, because communicating it to someone else implies taking some form of responsibility for its accuracy. There's no need to be perfectly certain about everything in life. If you are not entirely certain about a particular fact, you can provide a lot of value to other people by being forthcoming with that fact. And remember that if you can't answer the question, "How accurate is this information?" there is a good chance it might be bullshit.

Chapter Summary

- Most Geeks like to speak with complete openness and honesty, providing both high accuracy and high precision. This can be a challenge because it usually means including too much information for their audience. This approach is also difficult when you have an objective you need to achieve, because it can distract from it with unwanted details.
- Putting the best foot forward is another approach that emphasizes leading with points that are most positive and pertinent in the context of a particular objective. The core of this approach is to develop an elevator pitch that forms the basis for any discussion on the topic.
- This approach, however, only works to everyone's benefit when the audience takes responsibility to think and question what is said.
- Putting the best foot forward also requires a firm grasp on a complete understanding of the topic. If someone tried to put a statement in a positive light when it already has been put in a positive light, the result is usually bullshit.

- Lies, even small inconsequential ones, are extremely risky. They tend to fall apart over time, and undermine general trust in the speaker. If a lie makes a difference in how a message is perceived, it's not an inconsequential lie.
- Almost no one willingly says something that is bullshit, but it's very common to encounter it anyway.
- Bullshit usually happens when a speaker overestimates how accurate he or she is being. It also frequently happens when a message is repeated from person to person without any error correction.
- You can avoid this by constantly questioning yourself and checking the accuracy of what you are saying.

Chapter 16: Influencing people

Influence is a coveted commodity. Everyone wants it – to have influence is to have our thoughts and ideas valued by others. As I mentioned in Chapter 1, the goal of communicating effectively is to influence others, either by passively educating them or by selling them an idea.

The Elevator Pitch

One of the most important techniques we have to influence others is the "Elevator pitch". If you recall, this is a short, one sentence summary of what you want to say. The name comes from the following scenario: What would you say if you got in an elevator, and met someone that you wanted to convince of something before they got off on the second floor? In chapter 15, I explained how the elevator pitch calls for "putting the best foot forward" by offering a clear and positive summary of what's being said. Developing an elevator pitch is always the first step to creating a compelling message that can influence people.

If you've never tuned into Terry O'Reilly's 'Under the Influence' radio show on marketing, I highly recommend it. Terry O'Reilly is a highly influential voice in the marketing world. His weekly radio show is always entertaining and ripe with insights into how marketing affects us. In a recent show, he examined the topic of "Elevator pitches"[15]. Terry points out that marketing begins with the elevator pitch, and sometimes ends with the elevator pitch. If the pitch is clear and compelling, then the marketing campaign that follows it will be too. If the elevator pitch is confused or boring, then the resulting marketing will be so.

In the show, Terry also recounts the story of how John Sculley,

---

[15] http://www.cbc.ca/undertheinfluence/season-3/2014/04/05/elevator-pitches-1/

then president of Pepsi Cola, left to become CEO of the brand new Apple Computers. Steve Jobs pursued Sculley doggedly for months, calling him every few days, trying to entice him with money and over $50 million in stock options. But it was all to no avail, Sculley was fully committed to Pepsi. He said he "had it in his veins". Then finally, Jobs said one thing that made Sculley stop in his tracks, and change his mind. Jobs said, *Do you want to spend the rest of your life selling sugared water, or do you want a chance to change the world?*

It's important to understand, it wasn't the months of pursuit or the money that convinced Sculley. It was one poignant statement by Jobs that did. Jobs demonstrated that clarity is a powerful thing. It presents people with a simple choice: to agree with the statement or reject it.

I mentioned that in our start-up *xkoto*, we struggled at first with our sales pitches. Our complex and difficult to understand software was competing with several other products that *sounded* the same, but were much less advanced. Articulating why anyone would want to take a risk on our product was a challenge, until Roger, our Vice President of Sales, challenged us to come up with a clear elevator pitch. It was:

Our software delivers continuous availability, scalability and disaster recovery for your databases.

Developing this statement was a major turning point in our sales. All the customers we talked to needed the first item, *continuous availability*. Most wanted the second, *scalability*, but found it hard to justify the money to invest in it by itself. And the customers we talked to were already struggling (and sometimes failing) with the third, *disaster recovery*. Suddenly it was clear to everyone that our software provided not one or two, but three things they needed, and our conversations with them steadily improved. A clear elevator pitch not only helped the customers understand our product better – it helped us understand our product better. To this point, I had been reasonably skeptical about the future of our start-up. So many of our discussions focused on what seemed to be the wrong things. I also was simply being realistic; estimates vary, but as few as 1 in 4 to 1 in 10 IT start-ups actually turn into successful businesses. Most fail within 5 years. But Roger's statement provided me with a clear understanding of what we were working to achieve and it helped me realize that we had something of real value.

It doesn't always work out this way. Years after our start-up successfully *exited* by being acquired, a friend asked me to lunch to talk about a new product his company was developing. This product was going to take an innovative new approach on traditional IT monitoring products. Unfortunately, he was having a hard time developing an elevator pitch that explained how his product was different from existing products. He wondered if I could do any better. After thinking about it, I realized I couldn't either. Once the technology was explained to me, I understood that their product would be better than existing monitoring products. Nevertheless, I couldn't see any way to articulate this in a way that was concise and simple. It was just too hard to explain what was going to be different and compelling about the product. My friend left the lunch a little disappointed. This was a serious problem, since he would eventually need to pursue venture capital backing and one day pitch the product to customers. Later I learned his company had eventually abandoned the development of the new product to focus on other things. Without a compelling elevator pitch, a new technology doesn't have hope.

And an elevator pitch isn't just important for selling an IT product. It's also important for the engineers and developers building the product to hear and understand. It crystallizes the vision of what they are trying to achieve. In engineering terms, the elevator pitch could be called "The problem statement". Unfortunately, not all high-tech companies appreciate the importance of articulating a vision to their developers before they start working. It's a common mistake to assume that anything involving sales starts after the product has been built, not before.

Joining Objectives

The story about Steve Jobs' pitch to John Sculley provides insight because it demonstrates the need to unify the objectives of the audience with the objectives of the speaker. They should be one and the same. Steve Job's objective was to change the world. John Sculley wanted that too. Nevertheless, Sulley did not work with Jobs until he realized that he had the same objective as him.

Sales situations are good examples to explore the concept of a unified objective because on the surface, a sales transaction seems to involve two parties with irreconcilable objectives. Sales people want to sell products in exchange for money. Customers (usually) want to keep their money. But if the sales person can find a way to make the customer see that the product will solve a problem for him or her, then both of their objectives can be joined in a fair exchange.

Most people don't think of themselves in sales, but if you look closely at any human interaction, you'll see that we all engage in these little sales negotiations all the time. Any time you try to convince someone to give up something they value (E.g. their time) in return for something else, you are engaging in a form of sales. It could be a boss that is trying to motivate his employees, a significant other trying to convince you to take the time to clean up around the house, or a parent trying to coax his child into finishing her dinner.

Merging the audience's objectives and your own starts with thoroughly understanding what the audience's objectives are. Once these are understood, then you can begin to map each of your own objectives to the audience's. It's essential to do this as honestly as possible. If there is no genuine connection between what you want to achieve and what the audience is trying to achieve, then trying to pretend there is will not generate a compelling argument. Also, if you really don't believe there is a connection between your goals and the audience's, then the audience will probably not believe it either.

As an exercise, I recommend writing out in a table each of your audience's objectives. Then attempt to re-write your objectives to match that of the audience as closely as possible. For example, consider this conversation between a sales person selling IT monitoring software, and a potential customer:

Audience's objective: To increase its application uptime.
Speaker's objective: To sell monitoring software.

What's the shared goal of these two objectives? I'd suggest:

Shared objective: To help the customer figure out how monitoring software can increase his/her application uptime.

When preparing to speak to the customer, it's the shared objective that the sales person should be focused on. Their own goal of selling the software is actually secondary to achieving this. It should be ignored until the shared goal has been achieved, because once the shared goal has been achieved, it will follow automatically.

If the audience walks away from a sales presentation without that transformation from separate objectives into shared objectives, there is no sale. What's interesting about this is that it's not always obvious to the sales person if this magical transformation has occurred or not. Sometimes a sales person will be deluded into thinking that the audience was on the same page as them, when in reality it had no intention of buying the product. This sometimes happens because of a failure to uncover the audience's real objectives.

Ask, don't tell

Here's a wonderful way to convince an audience of a specific point. *Don't tell them it.* Tell them everything leading to it, laying out the bare facts, but leave out the conclusion. And then *ask them* what the conclusion is instead.

Letting the audience reach a conclusion through their own thinking is always far more compelling than telling it what it should think. There are two reasons for this. First, it encourages far more engagement from the audience than passively listening to what you have to say. By asking the audience to reach a conclusion, it needs to evaluate and take a stance on what was said so far. Second, once the audience reaches it, it firmly establishes the conclusion is the audience's as much as it is yours. People are much kinder in evaluating their own thinking than someone else's, and much more aggressive in defending it.

This can be a tricky gambit however, so it should be used with caution. If you remember from the last chapter, in general you should always try to lead with a conclusion, to avoid losing the audience's attention. But since this "ask, don't tell" technique requires the audience to reach the conclusion on its own, that's not possible. There is also a distinct danger that the audience may not reach the conclusion you want. This trick has been used twice in the US presidential race. It propelled Ronald Reagan to victory in 1980, when he asked the American people "Are you better off than you were four years ago?" In 1980, they didn't feel that they were better off, and wanted a change. But when Mitt Romney tried the same question in the 2012 US presidential election, it backfired. Americans did feel much better in 2012, coming out of a world-wide recession, than they did in 2008, going into one. They did not reach the conclusion Romney had wanted.

Finally, you should always keep in mind most audiences are fairly savvy and sensitive to any forceful attempt to influence them. If they perceive that you are trying to lead them into a conclusion, they may react negatively and stop listening to you altogether.

Timing is everything

In order to be effective, communication also needs to be timely. Too often, geeks tend to ignore the need to communicate with others until it's too late to contribute useful information. They tend to be passive and focused on their own activities, until they are forced to communicate. Effective communicators always try to convey the information they have to the people who need it, before they need it. But not too far in advance; otherwise they won't know what to do with the information they are given.

A perfect example to illustrate this is that of playing navigator while someone else drives a car. When you are giving someone else directions, you need to do it so they understand their next turn before it's too late to make it. To the driver, there's nothing as frustrating as hearing you should have made a turn, just as you zoom past the street you wanted. But conversely, it's also irritating and counterproductive to barrage the driver with information about multiple turns they will have to make far in advance. The next time you use a GPS in your car to navigate, you'll notice that it will tell you the next turn you need to make immediately after you complete the previous one, and then (regardless of the speed you are traveling), the GPS will remind you about an approaching turn 10-15 seconds before you need to make it. To do this, it takes into account the distance to the turn and how fast you are traveling, so the time to the turn remains a constant. This is critical to allow you to react in time, and it is not so far in advance that you will forget about it.

Obviously, if you want to direct someone towards a particular course of action, you need to state your case before the person has decided what to do. Sometimes, as in the last chapter with attempting to reach an audience that won't listen, this means changing your approach. Rather than waiting for someone to engage you in a conversation about a particular topic, during the critical point in time when they need to hear what you have to say about it, you can get ahead of the game. You do this by proactively getting your message on the topic out to a wide audience. This usually means changing the format of your message from a discussion to a written form. This method has an added advantage of potentially reaching more people who can relay what they have learned from your writing.

The trick with this approach is ensuring what you have written is referenced. Then when it becomes relevant to your audience, they will know about it and where to locate it. Naturally, the World Wide Web leads itself perfectly to this approach, since it makes it easy for people to publish and locate content on particular subjects.

This does not necessarily mean that when the time comes, you won't need the opportunity to discuss the topic with your target audience directly. It just helps ensures that they will be more aware of the existence of your message, and give a general idea of what your major points are. As we mentioned before, it's rare that someone will walk away from reading a document with the same understanding that he or she would have from a verbal conversation.

Timing also matters during a single conversation. As we saw in Chapter 3, sometimes irrational influences can impact how people perceive a message, and therefore how they make decisions. Additionally, it's been well studied that emotional states, group peer pressure, and simple physical urges like hunger, or the need to urinate can have a strong impact on the decisions we make. In *How to Meet the Queen*, Albert recounts one story of how chasing a potential investor into the bathroom helped launch our startup company, *xkoto*. Nevertheless, the effect of irrational influences is rarely evident to the person making the decision. Everyone instead likes to imagine he is perfectly rational, and the decisions he makes are well grounded in logic. The gap between this fallacy and reality is a vulnerability in our decision making processes. If your goal is to influence an audience then it must be carefully managed in order to obtain a fair assessment.

The Emperor's New Clothes

One of my favorite bedtime stories is "The Emperor's New Clothes". There's a vain ruler that is obsessed with having the fanciest clothes, and he's swindled by a pair of conmen into believing in an imaginary robe that is only visible to intelligent and gifted people. There's the hook – if you can't see the robe, you aren't intelligent and gifted. So the emperor lies and tells the conmen he can see the robe, and pays them a fortune for it. His advisors are similarly dragged by their own cowardice and insecurity into going along with the con. They won't admit to the emperor or each other that they can't see the robe. Finally the emperor parades the robe in front of the town people, who also can't bring themselves to contradict the consensus that the emperor's new clothes are spectacular. That is until one courageous and precocious little boy shouts in a crowd "He's not wearing any clothes!" And sure enough, once the truth is out there, everyone realizes what they've secretly suspected all along – that it was all a trick.

This tale is a favorite of mine for three reasons. It actually has a clear and relevant virtue behind it. Telling the truth is important if we don't want to be conned. A careful reading also suggests that telling the truth – for example, that we don't always see what we're told we are supposed to see, also requires courage. And finally, it illustrates that *consistency*, which as we've mentioned in chapter 5, our brains associate with truth, doesn't always align with social *consensus*.

But I also like this story because it's a fairy tale - an idealized story, separate from the realities of life. How could we make this story more realistic? The problem is the ending: the little boy exposes everyone's mistake, and then they all laugh about it and the emperor gets some real clothes on. How would you expect this story to end if the part of the emperor was played by Joseph Stalin, Adolf Hitler or Kim Jong-un? Men that become emperors tend to be a little sensitive about being laughed at. It definitely wouldn't end well for the little boy.

It's not just the emperor's error being exposed. It's his advisors, and the town's people. The official social consensus had clearly been established. Once the masses have accepted an idea, it can be very difficult to dissuade them. Galdwell's "Tipping Point" posits that masses of people tend to follow the lead of "mavens" – people that act as trend setters. Its maven's that start trends in fashion and other popular ideas. Mavens tend to be people with a high number of social connections, and high visibility. Would that description fit the little boy in the story? No, definitely not. So I'd suggest the most likely real-world ending to the "Emperor's New Clothes" is this: Everyone ignores the little boy, and the emperor continues to parade around naked until he catches a pneumonia and dies. Everyone in the town admits, in retrospect, that they all saw it coming, and the little boy, having grown up some, now feels jaded and cynical because no one listened to him.

What does this have to do with geeks, technology and influencing people? The first is the insight that genuine insights are disruptive. When an individual sees something that a group of people do not, they are going to face a very difficult time communicating the idea. In a business environment, this could be an innovative product idea, a plan for a better way of doing things, or an insight into how a product might fail. Technological innovation relies on disruptive ideas. Disruptive ideas come from free and open communication, so ideas can be shared. Social consensus suppresses open communication, so a smart leader in a technology organization that wants to innovate needs to create a safe environment that allows consensus to be challenged by open communication.

Here's another insight. Every few years, some new technology shakes up the IT industry. Industry analyses excitedly predict radical changes, tech magazines and trade shows buzz with excitement. Slick CTO's and CEO's take to the stage talking about the latest revolution set to change the world - the finest new technological clothes available for a reasonable price.

Don't get me wrong – occasionally, something new comes along that justifies a little hype. But more often than not, the fairy tale around a tool blows over, leaving a real-world shadow that is much more modest. If you have lived through enough of these hyped technologies, you begin to develop an appreciation of how short-lived these phases of hype can be – and how quickly technologies can come and go. COM, Java, C#, XML, Corba, .NET, JSON, SOAP, NoSQL, Columnar databases, Hadoop. Some have stuck around, but most die out. Most new technologies are examples of gradual change or niche problems becoming more main stream. Very few new IT technologies actually produce radical change. But for every hot new technology there tends to be a period when social consensus dictates that everyone must play along and not question its value. Individuals or companies that buck a trend risk looking out-of-touch. Not everyone can afford to do that.

A natural instinct when faced with social consensus that seems wrong is to directly and overtly challenge it - to act like the child in the Emperor's New Clothes, and call out the emperor, his advisors and everyone else. In real life, this approach usually doesn't very far. If a group's cognitive biases block receiving a new idea, then directly challenging them with a contrary idea will fail. Again, timing is everything.

So when open discussion or confrontation of an idea isn't effective, a more realistic approach is to be *subversive*. As illustrated by the examples of scientific and mathematical breakthroughs in Chapter 3, ideas are promiscuous. If one person looks at the world and reaches a conclusion, chances are there are others looking at the same world and reaching the same conclusion. The secret to changing social consensus on a topic is to find people with similar ideas and build a new consensus to subvert the old one. This is why individuals with a large number of social connections can trigger new trends. Often the individuals in a group will move away from a consensus quietly without voicing dissent. Then a maven, an individual with a high number of social connections, will trigger a new consensus by signaling the group that it's safe to start expressing the new idea. Suddenly, everyone will be talking about it and they will appear to have the influence to change the group's thinking. The reality is that it's the communication network that, in a literal sense, has the influence. The more effectively it works, the better ideas will spread.

Chapter Summary

- Writing an elevator pitch to summarize what you are trying to say is extremely important. It must be clear and compelling. If the elevator pitch doesn't work, or you can't come up with one, you will likely fail in convincing anyone with your statements.
- Try making a table listing all your objectives and the audience's objectives. Where possible, merge the two.
- Focus on the shared objectives of a conversation, and ignore any personal objectives until the shared ones are achieved.
- If you want to influence others into believing a particular point, lay out the case for that point, and then prompt them to draw a conclusion. It will be much more convincing if they reach the conclusion themselves. Be cautious in this approach however, because it can backfire if the audience disagrees with your conclusion or loses interest before they reach it.
- If you want to stay ahead of critical decisions, be proactive and pre-emptive with your communication by using written forms to get your message out.
- Genuinely new ideas are disruptive. They will be met with resistance and skepticism. They are also more valuable.
- Social consensus can suppress new ideas.
- Challenging social consensus can be risky. A more effective approach might be to subvert social consensus by reaching out to others and building a new social consensus.

Chapter 17: Confidence

In the techniques discussed in this book, I did not mention building confidence as a means to becoming a more effective communicator. There is a cult following, perhaps now in decline, of the notion that confidence is the key to all success in life. Unfortunately, the rationale behind much of this obsession with self-confidence has been proven to be ill-founded. Child psychologists now understand that providing a child with constant success and praise does not endow him or her with the ability to persist when facing a challenge. In fact, a child's over-confidence in his or her intelligence and abilities may actually limit that child's intellectual growth. A similar argument can be made about adults. Most successful people will tell you they learned to succeed through failing. This makes perfect sense — when you fail, you learn something. When you succeed, you only confirm what you already know.

Confidence is a nice feeling, but it's not a requirement to be an effective communicator, and may in fact be a hindrance. Confidence in communicating builds up naturally as you master techniques and see the results of that mastery. It's an end, not a means. When you do start to feel confidence, you should treat the feeling with caution. It can undermine your ability to communicate in several ways. The moment you are confident you understand what someone is saying, you stop listening to them. Confidence might also lead you to underestimate how much you need to prepare for a conversation, or how effective you are being at conveying your ideas to another person. Confidence is sometimes what you feel just before you screw something up.

Geeks should also realize that although they tend to have certain weaknesses in communication, non-geeks may have the same difficulties. People who identify themselves as Geeks tend to lack confidence in their communication skills because they realize they are not always listened to, and are at least partially marginalized by society. Geeks know they're not the cool kids. But many non-geeks also have seriously under developed communication skills, and might be oblivious to the fact. In my career, I've met many people in sales, management, teaching and other "people-centric" professions that were truly horrible communicators but did not realize it.

Thus, if you're a Geek, it's perfectly fine to not feel completely confident in your ability to communicate. In this regard, I believe Geeks need to cut themselves some slack. I believe we all have an unrealistic picture of what a great communicator looks like. Were you to ask a younger version of myself to name a great communicator, I'd probably pick someone like Martin Luther King, Franklin Roosevelt, or Winston Churchill. I, like most people, probably would have picked these people because they were all great orators and inspiring speakers. But consider the other hand — they were people that spoke on dramatic and emotional topics at pivotal points in history. They were and remain public icons. These are not the people we should look to as exemplary great communicators because they set some unrealistic standards. If you can deliver a speech like Martin Luther King, that's fantastic; I can't. But that doesn't mean I'm not a good communicator.

You do not need to be able to inspire people with a fiery speech to be an effective communicator either. Effective communication is not about swaying masses of people with emotion. It's about delivering a message in a manner so clear and simple that people understand it. You do not need to be as eloquent as Shakespeare or witty as Mark Twain (although it couldn't hurt), so we shouldn't compare ourselves to those figures as ideals. Instead, we should think about people like Fibonacci, whose ideas were picked up and have become so popular that it's hard to say where they came from. Remember that Fibonacci was nearly forgotten, not because he was not persuasive, but *because* he was so persuasive. His approach spawned numerous copies, and changed the world in the process.

Truth be told, introverts will always feel a little shy when they are thrust into roles involving communication. Some forms of communication, like writing, are definitely easier for introverts. But public speaking will always be a nerve-wracking experience. This is not a defect of personality or a character flaw; it's a consequence of brain structure and there is nothing wrong with it. A personal tendency towards caution has advantages as well as disadvantages, so it deserves some respect.

Introverts need to realize that bashfulness may influence their ability to communicate, but it does not *limit* their ability to communicate. It's sometimes hard to see, but how you feel about your own performance in a conversation often has little connection to how effective you really were. It depends on the perception of the audience and whether they found something of value in the exchange. There have been countless times I have underrated how well I performed delivering a message because I felt nervous or unsettled during the delivery, only to have someone in the audience tell me after that they thought it was fantastic. I also don't worry about hitting it out of the park the first time when I'm writing a document or giving a presentation. This is because, at heart, I'm a programmer. Whenever I write or talk on a topic, I give it a try, evaluate how it worked, fix the bugs, and then try it again. After a few dozen attempts, a topic that was tremendously difficult to discuss can become trivial. And figuring out what doesn't work and why it doesn't can be tremendously valuable.

Extroverts should be wary that their confidence in speaking to someone does not automatically mean they are brilliant communicators. They need to be even more cautious than introverts and ensure that they don't overestimate how well they are doing when they talk to someone. They need to be nervous about their overconfidence.

Being an effective communicator also does not require being a confident smooth talker. It certainly does not require the ability to tell a joke or make an audience fall in love with you. You don't always need to have an answer to every question, or be perfectly cool every time you address someone. You will also not necessarily feel "in your comfort zone" when you are trying to communicate with someone else. But that's not a bad thing; sometimes it's good to work outside the things you are comfortable with.

Chapter Summary

- Don't obsess about feeling confident when you are trying to communicate. Feeling confident is not the same thing as being

competent.
- When trying to improve your communication skills, don't compare yourself to unrealistic role models. You do not need to be a smooth talker or passionate speaker in order to be an effective communicator.
- Introverts should not underestimate their ability to communicate. Extroverts should not overestimate their ability.

Chapter 18: Conclusion

In a way, it's my hope that the audience for this book will someday disappear. That we, Geeks, and the people around us, will no longer marginalize "Geeks" as a distinct group that is somehow different because of its interests or passions. This would benefit everyone because it would mean the acceptance of people who are slightly different has become the norm. I believe this is a change that has already begun. Thanks to electronic gadgets and toys, we Geeks have captured the attention of the world. Now we need to do something with it. We need to realize that we can also be leaders. We have valuable contributions to make that go beyond smart phones and video games. To make these contributions, we Geeks need to reach out and talk to people, to make them understand why it's okay to be a little different. It's fun to study science, engineering, and every other cool thing geeks are passionate about.

At the beginning of the book, I mentioned the TV show "Big Bang Theory". It's notable that this isn't just a show about Geeks. The protagonists of the show are Geeks. They are the "heroes" of the show that the television audience is meant to laugh at, but also care about. This in itself is a bellwether of serious social progress, as was Bill Cosby's acting role in the 1980's. Cosby portrayed an upper-middle class, doctor and family man, who happened to be black. This showed that African Americans were finally being recognized as both likable and successful people in the United-States. Television is a great mirror of society.

There's a strong possibility that children growing up today might never consider themselves "Geeks" at all. You still might not be able to find someone who is physically close to you with similar interests, but today that's no longer a problem. Physical location has become irrelevant to socialization. People can now locate and interact with those people with the same interests around the world through the internet with almost no effort. There is no need for anyone to feel ostracized because they are different. In the future, geeks will just be normal people with passionate interests and full confidence in who they are. The world is becoming very small, but very deep. All of this will be thanks to the ability of Geeks to better communicate with each other.

Communicating is hard work. It's work because you need to constantly think about who you are trying to reach, how they are thinking, and what you can use to bridge the gap between your brain and theirs. It means using techniques like repetition, careful word choices, and a common language to achieve your objectives. It requires controlling influences that might lead to irrational connections in the brains of your audience, recognizing that while people strive to be rational, they are stuck with neural wiring that is partially irrational. It requires getting in someone else's head to interpret their perspective, and what he or she wants to get out of a conversation. It also requires extending respect to your audience, and realizing that if you need to simplify your message, it's not because your audience is not as smart as you, it's because it just happens to not know what you know. You need to pick the right level of detail for each person in your audience

As with all work, you will sometimes get tired of doing this. It's not something you can do constantly without taking a break. In my job, I have two distinct modes, one for when I'm communicating and one for working by myself. Switching between these modes requires some effort, and judging which mode I need to be in when I'm working with someone requires some mental focus. And there are times I don't get it right. Due to lack of time or patience, I sometimes miss the opportunity to communicate with someone because I'm too focused on the task at hand. Like all failures, it's good to acknowledge your errors so you can learn from them. But you should never beat yourself up over your mistakes because that leads to self-defeat.

It's also hard to constantly be in "communication mode" because sometimes you don't have clear objectives. Effective communication requires preparation to clearly understand your objective — what you need to cover and what order you need to cover it in. Sometimes you don't have all that information. Sometimes you need to talk things out to realize what it is you have to say. As we discussed before, that's perfectly fine. It's a good idea in these circumstances to be clear about that uncertainty. Engage your audience to participate in your thought process by explicitly telling them you're not sure about the topic.

Communicating with others can be tiring because it requires constant self-awareness. You need to constantly ask yourself questions like, "Am I really listening?" and, "Have I given the audience a chance to respond?" as well as "How accurate is what I am saying?" and, "Am I giving too much detail, or too little?". There are a lot of questions to deal with. On top of these, we all have tendencies towards certain attitudes, limited patience, pride, vanity, laziness and prejudice, which need to be recognized if we are to overcome them.

In spite of the effort involved, building the skills needed to become an effective communicator is tremendously valuable. If you are a geek working in a role involving science, engineering, or almost anything else involving thinking, then you probably rely heavily on your ability to communicate with others. You may not be consciously aware of it, but the ideas that appear in your head likely came from someone else via some form of communication. By becoming more aware of how this communication occurs, you can enhance it. You can become more receptive to receiving new ideas, and make your ideas easier for others to pick up.

This allows you to achieve far more than you could by yourself. It is by engaging other people with ideas that the world can be transformed. We need geeks to transform the world, not just by producing the next electronic gadget or scientific breakthrough, but by teaching, guiding and leading. Everyone will benefit if geeks and non-geeks communicate efficiently with one another and develop the common objective of improving the planet we live on.

Bibliography

- Lee, Albert - *How to Meet the Queen - Ask Good Questions, Get Good Answers* – Nilwall Group – ISBN 978-9880406-0-1

- Buonomano, Dean - *Brain Bugs - How the brain's flaws shape out our lives* - W.W. Norton & Company, Inc.; ISBN 978-0-393-07602-8

- Cain, Susan - *Quiet - The Power of Introverts in a world that can't stop talking* - Publisher: Crown Publishing Group; ISBN 0-307-35214-5

- Gladwell, Malcolm - *The Tipping Point -How little things can make a big difference* - Publisher: Little Brown; ISBN 0-316-34662-4

- Henderson, Mark - *The Geek Manifesto - Why Science Matters* - Publisher: Corgi; ISBN-10: 0552165433

- Steven D. Levitt and Stephen J. Dubner - *Super Freakanomics - Global Cooling, Patriotic Prostitutes, and Why Suicide Bombers Should Buy Life Insurance* - Publisher: William Morrow; ISBN: 0-06-088957-8

- Shulman, Seth - *The Telephone Gambit - Chasing Alexander Graham Bell's Secret* – Publisher: W.W. Norton & Company, Inc.; ISBN: 039333368X

- Devlin, Keith - **Man of Numbers:** *Fibonacci's Arithmetic Revolution* - Publisher: Walker Publishing Co. 2011. *ISBN 978-0-8027-7812-3*

- Mandell, Terri - *Power Schmoozing - The new Etiquette for social and business success* - Publisher: McGraw-Hill; 1 edition (July 1 1996) ISBN-10: 0070398879

- Bruno Gideon – *Don't take No for an Answer* – Publisher: Matterhorn Publishing; ISBN 0-9732491-1-0

Acknowledgements

I'd like to thank my editor John Dias for his hard work and dedication in making this book happen. His fresh perspective, hard work, insight and enthusiasm were invaluable in the making of this book.

I've been extremely lucky to have excellent mentors over the years that have guide me to polish my communication skills. Albert Lee was always a fount of sage and insightful advice, both in business and in life. Roger Walker endured countless hours in my company on the road, while teaching me the fine art of sales. I've had countless technical mentors that have helped me build my technical skill set. I'd specifically like to thank Mark Peters, Dr. Jeff Heisz, and David LaPointe for fostering my technical development over the years.

I'd like to thank the late Graham Smyth, an exceptional teacher and human being, for first teaching the ins and outs of office politics and how to rise above them to focus on real values.

I'd like to acknowledge my first and most influential teacher, my father, James LaPointe, who could communicate volumes with a single raised eyebrow.

The majority of this book was written while sitting in airports waiting for flights. I owe a debt of gratitude to our airline industry for making me wait so long I had time to write a book. In particular, I'd like to thank Chicago O'Hare for the endless hours of productivity away from home.

Finally, this book would not be possible without the love and support of my wonderful wife Sharon.

About the Author

Paul LaPointe is an IT Solution Architect working for Teradata Labs in Toronto, Canada, where he lives with his lovely wife Sharon and their energetic daughter Aurora. Paul is a former database developer and administrator, and has spoken at numerous industry events, like *IBM's Information On Demand*, and Teradata's *Partner's*.

In 2005, he was part of a motley crew of geeks that formed the innovative start-up *xkoto*, headed by Albert Lee. During that time, Paul worked with the best and brightest at IBM and Microsoft to deliver customer solutions based on xkoto's patented technology. Paul helped develop the technical sales approach that helped xkoto successfully exit after a five year journey to become part of Teradata.

In his spare time, Paul is an active wood-worker, raspberry (the berry) micro-farmer, raspberry Pi (the computer) enthusiast, open source developer and general tinkerer.

To get in touch with Paul, please email **paul.lapointe@gmail.com**.

Contacting the Editor

John Dias is a narrative and non-fiction editor, based in Toronto, Canada. In addition to serving as the sports editor for the news publication *The Underground* and the senior editor of the creative writing anthology *Scarborough Fair*, he is also the author of six published short stories and several journalistic articles.

John can be reached at: johnjdias@live.com

Made in the USA
Lexington, KY
29 July 2018